'Yours Ever, Charlie'

'Yours Ever, Charlie'

A WORCESTERSHIRE SOLDIER'S JOURNEY TO GALLIPOLI

ANN CROWTHER

The
History
Press

❧ DEDICATION ❧

This book is dedicated to the memory of my father Wilfred (or Tim, as he was almost universally known), a little boy who had to grow up too fast and become the family breadwinner at the age of ten. To his eternal credit he waived his own dreams and set out to get the best possible education for his four younger siblings, three of whom went to grammar school. His oldest sister, Marjorie, was an outstanding school student and was only prevented from going to Cambridge (or any other university or college) by the sheer lack of money. She qualified as a teacher the hard way, working long years before she was able to qualify, yet she was held in great respect far and wide as an inspiration, and eventually had a spell as Acting Headmistress of Wilden School, where she spent almost all her working life.

First published 2010

The History Press
The Mill, Brimscombe Port
Stroud, Gloucestershire, GL5 2QG
www.thehistorypress.co.uk

© Ann Crowther, 2010

The right of Ann Crowther to be identified as the Author
of this work has been asserted in accordance with the
Copyrights, Designs and Patents Act 1988.

ISBN 978 0 7524 5528 0

Typesetting and origination by The History Press
Printed in Great Britain
Manufacturing managed by Jellyfish Print Solutions Ltd

Contents

About the Author

Ann Crowther was born in rural Worcestershire in 1938, growing up in the little village of Wilden. From early schooldays her twin passions have been music and history, and these were pursued vigorously at Sheffield University where she read Modern Constitutional History and Comparative Government while spending far too much time on various musical activities! After a brief period teaching history, Ann has spent the years singing and teaching singing. She lives on Merseyside with her husband, Michael, and currently juggles a busy voice-coaching practice, a prizewinning youth chamber choir, a University of the Third Age choir, and a somewhat fair-weather passion for gardening. She has one son and a small grandson.

Acknowledgements

I have been most fortunate to have had friends around me who have both encouraged me and helped in the gathering of information and in putting my book together; in particular, Richard Walker gave me some very sound advice when I first began. Maggie Herbert has been tireless in rooting out possible photographs and archive material, while Nicola Guy of The History Press has been a huge support and patience personified. HarperCollins generously allowed me to use a map from their 2009 road atlas, which should be useful to those wanting to pinpoint the various small places which feature in the text. Richard Cory, grandson of Canon W.H. Cory, has been a mine of information and has given me access to several crucial photographs from his family archive; chatting to him has been a wonderful way of jogging the memory. Elizabeth Bramhall has done a great job in paring down some very complicated maps in order to give readers a clear idea of the locations where Charles fought. I am indebted to Nic Harvey for his generosity of spirit in sharing some of his own researches on Wilden's past, and for his friendship. I am also indebted to Mike J. Bourne and Arthur Jones for many snippets of valuable information about Wilden and some of the people in this book.

Jean Talbot of the Kidderminster Carpet Museum Trust Archive Centre has been tremendously helpful and has dug out some very useful material; she has also been a patient sounding board for lines of research. Like so many of the people who have helped me, she and her colleagues are devoted volunteers. My grateful thanks go to Colonel John Lowles and his fellow volunteers at the Worcestershire Regiment Museum Trust. Colonel Lowles has set me right over numerous problems of military detail, and has given me access to Captain H. FitzM Stacke's seminal account, *The Worcestershire Regiment in the Great War*. He also gave me permission to use three precious photographs of the Worcestershire Regiment in Gallipoli. The wonderful photographs of the Wilden Church windows come by courtesy of photographer and artist the late Ray Carpenter, my childhood friend and one-time Head Boy of Wilden Church Choir under Harry Oakes. Ray very generously made those and two of his paintings of Wilden available to me, and filled in some vital small details.

Lovely Al Murray produced his excellent foreword within a week of being asked, despite being at the beginning of a gruelling national tour (Al is godfather to Charles' great-great-grandson). My grateful thanks go also to Tony Higginson of Pritchard's Bookshop in Formby, on Merseyside. He has been my creative writing and world of publishing guru, my unofficial agent, my tower of strength and my friend. I owe a huge debt of gratitude to Earl Baldwin of Bewdley, great-grandson of Alfred Baldwin; he graciously allowed me the use of a drawing and two photographs from his family albums. One of the photographs is of my great-grandfather, William, and is the only verified one in existence, which none of my family had ever seen until now; this has been a real treasure trove! I am hugely appreciative of my cousin, Sue Gardner's support; she has borne many hours of listening to my obsession, and has been my companion on many quests for information. Like me, she is Charles' granddaughter. Finally, my undying thanks to my husband Mike, who has scanned letters, sharpened photographic images, proof-read, and generally made the work of this IT rookie rather more professional.

I very much hope that there will be a knock-on effect upon the Worcestershire Regiment Museum Trust, on Wilden Church, and on the Kidderminster Carpet Trust Archive Centre. All three are served by devoted volunteer staff without whom they would not survive.

Foreword

by Al Murray

The First World War is an event that, as it becomes more distant from us historically, becomes clearer to see, yet even harder to understand. That it was the catalytic event of the twentieth century and that we are still living with its consequences is without doubt. Debate about how it began, how the world was tipped into a chasm of unprecedented slaughter goes on; how politicians let go the reins of order and let loose chaos has been the subject of nearly a century of discussion, but at its heart lie many compelling mysteries. If it is true that the war was the greatest catastrophe to befall the world, why was it allowed to continue? If the war was Europe's first great war fought by entire populations, fought by ordinary men, why did the ordinary men fight even as they died in unprecedented numbers? Maybe one way to answer this is to perhaps ask, as best we can, the ordinary men who fought in the First World War, by reading their letters and their diaries.

In some senses the First World War has also gone beyond being a merely historic event, it has become an iconic cultural episode. It lives in art, film and music, in national self-perception. The Battle of Gallipoli – which is where Charles Crowther was wounded – is, rightly, seen in Australia and New Zealand as a central, defining moment in their national history, being the first time that the Australia and New Zealand Army Corps – the Anzacs – had fought. It is also a key moment in Turkish national history. However, it is often overlooked that twice as many British soldiers as Anzacs were killed in the battle, and that at the time the landings in the Dardanelles were viewed by many as a daring and essential operation to speed up an Allied victory.

Conceived by Winston Churchill, the First Lord of the Admiralty, the landings at Gallipoli were intended to knock Germany's ally, Turkey, out of the war by capturing Constantinople (now Istanbul) and secure a sea route to Russia. As the war had become static on the Western Front with both sides stalled and dug in, Churchill became convinced that the deadlock could be broken on the periphery and that Turkey's enemies, Bulgaria and Greece, would be drawn into the war on the Allied side. The landings were delayed, giving the Turks time to prepare their defences. From April 1915 through to January 1916, the Allied troops clung onto their beachhead, the fighting fierce throughout, with the casualties amounting to around 42,000 Allied soldiers killed and another 97,000 wounded. The Turks lost even more. When the Allies withdrew from Gallipoli they did so in abject failure – Churchill's political career was virtually ruined and Turkey remained on the German side.

That's the broad picture, but for each of the men there was their personal, individual experience. Amidst the mind-boggling numbers from the First World War, it can be easy to forget each of these men, their family and their friends. This book is about one of these men, his family and his friends as he makes his own, ultimately tragic, journey through the war. It perhaps takes us closer to understanding why men went to war, what sustained them in unimaginably hard times, and how they thought they were doing the right thing.

Al Murray: comedian, historian and presenter of *Al Murray's Road to Berlin*.

Introduction

The inspiration for this book sprang from the letters which my grandfather, Charles Crowther, wrote to my grandmother, Dora Kate, in the latter part of 1915 and January 1916, as he made the swift transition from a wounded, over-age soldier in a reserve battalion to a front-line infantryman in a replacement battalion fighting in Gallipoli. As I pored over the letters, which contain so many references to family, home and village life, I began to feel the need to expand my canvas; here was a chance to reveal the whole man and attempt to understand why loving family men like Charles actually volunteered to go to war in 1914.

Charles was the second of seven children in a close and devoted family. He was born in 1871, a year after his parents moved to the little Worcestershire village of Wilden, almost halfway between Kidderminster and Stourport-on-Severn. Before the move, generations of Crowthers had lived just across the Severn. His mother, Eliza, came from a Herefordshire family, the Lippetts, who farmed land near Leominster. At the age of twenty-one, Eliza went to work as a cook for an affluent Worcestershire farmer near the village of Shrawley. The farmer also employed a personable young groom called William Crowther. The two soon fell in love and were married some years later. William's family lived in Shrawley and had connections with three of the other villages which circle the great house of Witley Court at Great Witley, namely Astley, Martley, and Pensax. It was a hugely fertile farming area, which provided a great deal of employment both in field and house.

Ambitious and hard-working young people like William and Eliza, doing their sort of jobs, were constantly in contact with merchants, rich farmers and industrialists who had good work opportunities to offer. Their big opportunity came around 1864, when they met Alfred Baldwin, a young man who was their own age. From that moment Eliza, William and Alfred were bound together for the rest of their lives, and soon they were to include Alfred's wife, Louisa Macdonald, whom he married in 1866, at which point Eliza and William went to work for Alfred. William remained employed by the Baldwins for fifty-seven years, until he died in 1924. Ties of affection and mutual respect continued between Alfred's son, Stanley (a future Prime Minister), and William's children. Much later, William's granddaughter, Marjorie, was an indefatigable constituency worker for Stanley during the latter part of his political career. William's son, Charles, was a pall-bearer at Alfred's funeral, and Charles' son, Wilfred, was a pall-bearer at Stanley's. Duty and readiness to be of service were driving forces in lives such as theirs.

Charles was fatally wounded at Gallipoli on 29 November 1915, just before the evacuation of British troops began. He was taken by sea to Malta where he was nursed in the Royal Naval Hospital at Bighi, above the village of Kalkara. By the beginning of February 1916, he was dead, leaving a widow and five small children, aged from five months to nine years old. He never saw the baby, Louisa. He was buried with full military honours in the Royal Naval Cemetery at Bighi.

Before he was sent to Gallipoli, Charles had already fought and been wounded in France early in 1915. For his efforts during that fateful year he received the 1914-15 Star, the Military Medal, the Distinguished Conduct Medal and the Silver War Badge. He was also 'mentioned in dispatches.' According to my father, nothing came of a proposed medal citation for bravery because all his immediate commanding officers were killed; I suspect that this is true of many reports of bravery. It has been very difficult to trace his movements in France; the Battle of Aubers Ridge where he was probably wounded was a catastrophe amid massive confusion, and his name does not appear on the Worcestershires' list of wounded. I have had to make some guarded assumptions about what occurred.

I have always had a head full of family history. My father, Wilfred, never really came to terms with the death of the father he worshipped, and talked endlessly of him and of family and friends in the past. I remember as a child being hugely embarrassed on Remembrance Sundays when he would stand in church, crushing me to his side, weeping as Bill Calcott dipped the British Legion flag in front of the War Memorial plaque. How little the young understand! Later on, as a teenager, I came to find Remembrance Sunday services intensely moving and it was always a struggle to keep singing to the end of 'O Valiant Hearts'. To my father it was always like yesterday, with vivid recollections. Thanks to him I have been able to build up a picture of Charles, my grandmother and their life. My father's love for my grandmother was deep and sometimes almost reverential; I never once heard him refer to her as 'Mother'. To him she was always Dora Kate. Dora Kate was indeed a very special and stately lady. One uncle (my mother's much younger brother) remembers meeting her as a young boy and being 'scared stiff' of such a dignified person; she died when I was six, but I still have fleeting memories of a warm, loving grandmother with a big jar of mint imperials under her bed.

The most amazing thing about assembling this book has been the jigsaw effect as snippets of childhood memories and my father's inexhaustible fund of family anecdotes slotted themselves into little gaps which I had not expected to fill. So many fragmented pieces of information, dormant in my head for most of my adult life, finally erupted and made sense. I think my father's wide knowledge of family background was largely due to the amount of time he spent with his grandfather after the death of his father when he was nine. William's duties were light by then, and he had plenty of time for Wilfred. Dora Kate's brother-in-law, William Bourne, was also very influential, because Charles had been his best friend, and he loved to talk to Wilfred about him.

My husband and I have visited Malta twice so far, and paid our respects to my grandfather; the first time was just before 11 November 1995 and I was able take him flowers and a poppy cross. I have to say that the first time I visited his grave I was overwhelmed by the thought of being only 6ft away from his remains, and yet unable to touch him.

I wept for a long time at the waste of life, the missed opportunities, and for a daughter and grandchildren he never saw. The Naval Cemetery where he lies is beautifully kept and treated with great respect. By a rare coincidence Nurse Glover, one of the staff at the hospital where Charles died on Malta, came from Hartlebury, the nearest village to Wilden, Charles' home. She had known Charles' sister, Alice, who was Headmistress of Hartlebury Village School. Nurse Glover and her colleagues were extremely kind, not only making all the funeral arrangements and taking photographs of the grave with its flowers, but also keeping up a correspondence with Alice for a long time afterwards. That link and kindness meant a great deal to my grandmother; he had made a deep impression on the hospital staff, to the extent that one of the nurses used to bake scones especially for him, because he loved them so. Everyone seems to have liked Charles and they admired him, found him interesting and applauded his courage and dignity.

THE CROWTHERS 1868-1915

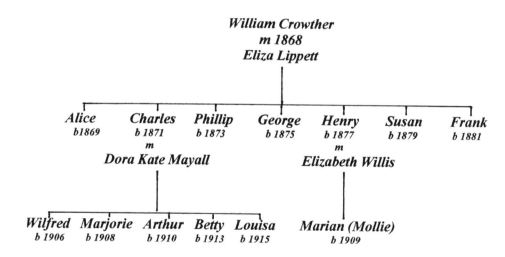

This simplified family tree shows the relationships between the Crowthers in this book.

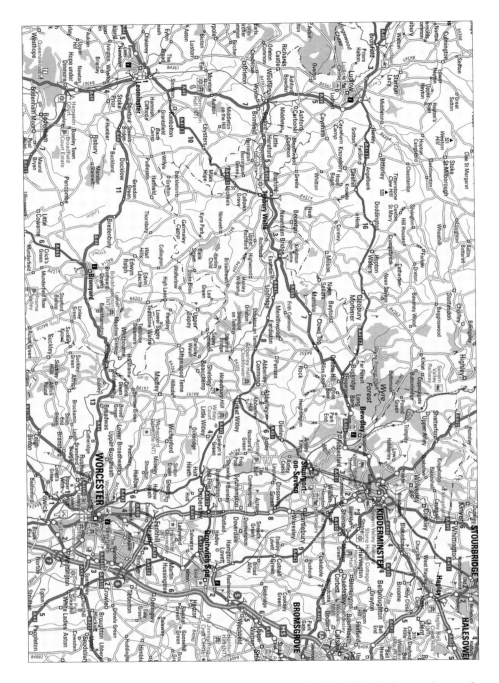

Above Shrawley, Pensax, Martley, Astley, Bewdley, Stourport and Wilden all circle the great house of Witley Court at Great Witley. On the left is the spa town of Tenbury Wells. (Courtesy of HarperCollins, copyright 2009)

Opposite This is one of Rudyard Kipling's best-known poems; many who knew him and his cousin, Stanley Baldwin, strongly believed that he wrote this poem about Stanley. It is also very pertinent to men like Charles Crowther.

❧ I F ❧

(Rudyard Kipling)

If you can keep your head when all about you
Are losing theirs and blaming it on you,
If you can trust yourself when all men doubt you,
But make allowance for their doubting too;
If you can wait but not be tired by waiting,
Or being lied about, don't deal in lies,
Or being hated, don't give way to hating,
And yet don't look too good, not talk too wise;

If you can dream – and not make dreams your master;
If you can think – and not make thoughts your aim;
If you can meet with Triumph and Disaster
And treat those two impostors just the same;
If you can bear to hear the truth you've spoken
Twisted by knaves to make a trap for fools,
Or watch the things you gave your life to, broken,
And stoop and build 'em up with worn-out tools:

If you can make one heap of all your winnings
And risk it all on the turn of pitch-and-toss,
And lose, and start again at your beginnings
And never breathe a word about your loss;
If you can force your heart and nerve and sinew
To serve your turn long after they're gone,
And so hold on when there is nothing in you
Except the Will which says to them: 'Hold on!'

If you can talk with crowds and keep your virtue.
Or walk with Kings – nor lose the common touch,
If neither foes nor loving friends can hurt you,
If all men count with you, but none too much;
If you can fill the unforgiving minute
With sixty seconds' worth of distance run,
Yours is the Earth and everything that's in it,
And – which is more – you'll be a man, my son!

The artist has kept the left-hand side of the lane clear in order to show off the works; there were cottages facing across the road which are not drawn in. Wilden House juts right down to the road; it had two wings at right angles to each other. The coach house is not accurately shown, and was just beyond the point where the road curved around Wilden House.

The artist, Plowden, must have been sitting outside the coach house to draw this Wilden scene in 1935. He was looking back at Wilden House and the works. The main reason for demolishing Wilden House in the late 1930s after Louisa Baldwin and her sister, Edith, were both dead was the urgent need to widen the road in order to cope with rapidly-developing motor transport. The coach house was removed to make way for an office car park.

❦ PART ONE ❦

Chapter One

Wilden

Charles Crowther's parents, William and Eliza, went to work for Alfred Baldwin in 1866, when Alfred married Louisa Macdonald. Eliza, William and Alfred had met two or three years earlier when William and Eliza were first 'walking out' and working for an Astley farmer. Alfred was idealistic, God-fearing and had a strong social conscience; he came from a family of iron founders with many business interests in the area. William was a groom with good looks, charm and the beginnings of an impressive personality. He and Eliza went to live in with Alfred Baldwin and his wife when they set up home in an elegant house in nearby Bewdley (roughly four miles from the Baldwin Ironworks in Wilden). William was still a groom, but it would seem that he was being trained to take over as coachman. Also taken on at the same time was a delightful woman called Emma Payne, who worked as cook to Alfred's household from 1866 until her death in 1894; her verbal eccentricities were a source of great entertainment to staff and employers alike, so much so that Louisa wrote many of Emma's sayings down in a special notebook.

In 1868 William and Eliza were married from the Bewdley house, in the beautiful old church in nearby Ribbesford. Some years later, Alfred's nephew, Rudyard Kipling, would also be married at Ribbesford. William spent fifty-seven years in the employment of Alfred and Louisa Baldwin, and for some unexplained reason, was always known as Bobo to Alfred and his wife, and also to his only son, Stanley, and his children. The two men were the same age and were lifelong friends. William's first child, Alice, was born in the Bewdley house in 1869, two years after the birth of Stanley. The house is now resplendent with a Blue Plaque proclaiming the birthplace of a British Prime Minister.

In 1870, Alfred took over the ownership and management of his family's ironworks in Wilden. There had been years of mismanagement and Alfred sorted matters out at his own expense and took over the running of the works, which had been Baldwin-owned since 1840. With the exit of his two much older brothers from the works and village, Alfred was able to move his own little family into Wilden House, the main Baldwin residence in the village. William was now promoted to the post of coachman, and Alfred installed him and his little family in the lovely old coach house across the lane, opposite the Wilden House gates, with stables to the rear and plenty of room for growing vegetables and fattening pigs for winter. Here William and Eliza eventually had six more children, including Charles. William's fortnightly wage was two guineas, a generous payment. (The outgoing coachman earned £1 16s.)

One wing of Wilden House came right down to the narrow village lane; another wing, at right-angles to it, sat across the site atop a slope, and with a higher roof-line. Access on foot was straight up a steep path with steps; William would take the coach across the road, through the gateway and veer sharp right, following a curved drive which swept round the edge of the grounds and which helped the wheels to grip in bad weather. Much later, when the Baldwins bought a car and employed a chauffeur, Sam Jay, he took the same route which William had used. It is amusing to note that Sam Jay's family kept the public house close to the Wilden House gates, rather grandly known as the King of Prussia; it was hurriedly renamed the Wilden Inn in 1914 when hostilities broke out. (After William and Eliza died, Sam Jay and his wife moved into the coach house for a while.)

Wilden was a pleasant and sprawling village, with a few farms and the Baldwin ironworks. It lay in an agricultural area with views of several of the hill ranges that circle that part of north-west Worcestershire. The population in 1880 was 367, living in seventy-one households. Most of the homes lay along the eastern side of the one main street, Wilden Lane, which was over a mile long. On the other side of the road was the River Stour, at first running close behind the works, then looping away from the road to run around Wire Mill Farm, and then beside the Sling footpath to the bottom of a steep drop as the road went uphill; a couple of miles later it joined the River Severn at Stourport. Only the works, the coach house and a handful of cottages lay on the Stour side of Wilden Lane. Behind the houses, along the developed side, rose a red, sandstone ridge with three steep lanes leading up to the top of it, where another road, Wilden Top, ran parallel to the main street. The village has Domesday references, and Wilden had been home to one of seven wire mills strung along the banks of the small yet deep and fast-flowing River Stour in early times. The ironworks was a development of the ancient Wilden wire mill site. At one point in the previous century there had been as many as seventeen mills powered by the twenty-four-mile stretch of the little Stour, which sprang up in the Clent Hills.

The ironworks was linked to the nearby Staffordshire & Worcestershire Canal by means of Platt's Wharf, an ingenious method of purposely flooding the Stour. Originally the Stour ran through the works, driving water wheels. By Alfred's time, the Stour was diverted to run behind the works. A short stretch of canal had been dug between the works and the road, leading to a store yard, with a link onto the Stour. Barges laden with coal slack and iron bars came down the Staffordshire & Worcestershire Canal and, by means of a lock, were fed onto the Stour once it was flooded. The barges were floated downstream and unloaded into the store yard; their contents could be taken on the short stretch of Wilden Canal into the heart of the works as required, again by barge. The finished rolled metal was then taken back to the store yard by barge and loaded onto carts and, by the twentieth century, lorries for transporting by road. The works prospered under Alfred. It was the hub of village life.

In common with other notable industrial philanthropists of the Victorian age, Alfred was anxious to improve the quality of life in his village. Charles and his siblings witnessed momentous developments in the village as they grew from childhood into their teens. The arrival of a bevy of very talented people in Wilden did much to fire the imagination and the feeling of living in a special place; lack of knowledge of any other community sharpened the focus on local loyalties. Alfred built both a new school and a church for Wilden. He built the school in 1882 and extended it eight years later; it still flourishes today. Charles' oldest daughter, Marjorie, spent almost her entire working life teaching at the school, and I began my education there. The need for a church had become pressing. All births, marriages and deaths were registered in nearby Hartlebury and burials had to be there, so Wilden needed its own church and a burial ground. In addition, boundary changes made by the Ecclesiastical Commissioners now left Wilden somewhat isolated. Alfred set about providing both a church and burial ground and quickly gained approval from the Ecclesiastical Commissioners. Land was acquired, plans were drawn up, builders engaged and an organ ordered from a London firm of organ builders. Alfred said that he wanted his church to be 'a miniature cathedral in a village'; to that end, he set aside a generous amount of money in order to attract the finest musician possible to be organist and choirmaster. The first organist, F.A. Griffiths, held the post briefly and was followed by his nephew. \J. Irving Glover FRCO. 'Jig' Glover was a successful, published hymn writer, and conductor of Kidderminster Music Society and of Kidderminster Choral Society (1899-1932).He was succeeded at Kidderminster Choral Society and at Wilden by Harry Oakes FRCO, a brilliant organ scholar under C. Hubert Parry at the Royal College of Music and, for a while, Chorus Master of what is now the CBSO Choir. Harry Oakes might have had a national career had he not come back from war in 1918 seriously suffering from the effects of mustard gas. One of his 1949 concerts with KCS lived long in memory, being an unforgettable performance of Edward Elgar's *Gerontius* with Heddle Nash and a young Kathleen Ferrier. The music at Wilden was of a standard unheard of in a small village church and was further aided by a generous budget for the purchase of sheet music. Alfred's money enabled Wilden Church to acquire a music library for its choir that most large city churches would have envied. The Baldwin family added many gifts to garnish the church, in particular, 'The Baldwin Silver'. This was a gift from Louisa, and was a Communion plate, chalice and jug in silver and set with some of her own personal jewels. The silver is now kept in the bank, but is brought out from time to time for public viewing. In the early days William would carry the Communion set from Wilden House to the church on a tray covered by a snowy white, linen cloth.

All Saints, Wilden, was consecrated in May 1880 and was at first a Chapel of Ease, attached to St Michael's in Lower Mitton, Stourport. In 1896 William Henry (Harry) Cory was appointed as Curate in Charge. He was a thirty-year-old Cambridge graduate from Ely, fluent in Latin and Greek, and a potential high-flier within the Church. He had been recommended to Alfred by Canon Newbolt, who had been the Principal of Ely Theological College when Harry Cory was studying there. In 1904 Alfred Baldwin produced extra funds to endow the church and Wilden was made a parish; Harry Cory was now appointed Vicar of Wilden and Alfred built a splendid vicarage. The Reverend

Cory embraced life in Worcestershire and married Phoebe, daughter of Alfred's ironworks' manager, William Felton. He became editor of the *Diocesan Gazette* and then of the *Diocesan Directory*; in 1936 he was made an Honorary Canon of Worcester Cathedral. One may wonder why such a man stayed in Wilden until his retirement in 1948, but his family have always known that he stayed for Phoebe's sake, for she loved Wilden and was surrounded there by the large and loving Felton family whom she could not bear to leave. There is no doubt that Alfred chose well when he sought men to serve his church and the village of Wilden, who could promote his ideals and be looked up to as role models.

The true glory of Wilden Church is, without doubt, its collection of fourteen stained-glass windows designed by Alfred's brother-in-law, Edward Burne Jones, and there is probably not another church anywhere in which all the glass is by William Morris. The little church is alight with Burne Jones' saints and angels, all dedicated to Alfred and those close to him. Sad to say, the space for Louisa Baldwin's memorial window was never filled with her chosen figure of St Margaret of Scotland; she had sat with Burne Jones early on and chosen from his designs to reflect her Scottish ancestry. By the time Louisa died, William Morris' old firm had ceased to exist and to quote Windham Baldwin, her grandson, 'it was deemed wrong to proceed to match with modern means the matchless stained glass lines which were his own special glory.' Thus, Louisa's window, placed beside the figure of Joshua, dedicated to Alfred in 1909, contains simple Burne Jones 'foliage' created years before by Morris.

The collaboration between Burne Jones and Morris was part of a unique coming together of outstanding artistic talents within the extended Baldwin family. Alfred's wife, Louisa, had four sisters, three of whom married well, like herself. One married John Lockwood Kipling and was the mother of Rudyard. One married Sir Edward Poynter, President of the Royal Academy. The other married Sir Edward Burne Jones. All were beautiful, and they were a close and affectionate family. Within the world of the arts, contacts were legion. There were many comings and goings of talented and famous people; and all the time, Alfred and his 'forge' prospered and Wilden benefited.

In later life, Stanley Baldwin would say of the Wilden of those times that it was 'a place where from childhood I had known every man and could talk to each about problems at work or at home.' He remembered Wilden as a place where strikes were unheard of, and generation after generation went into the works. No one ever got the sack, and there was a natural sympathy for those less concerned with efficiency 'than this modern generation is.' There were large numbers of old gentlemen who sat around on wheelbarrow handles, smoking their pipes. However, the works was not inefficient; in the iron industry its expertise was second to none, and major awards were won. At the Paris Exhibition in 1878, Wilden Works won the only Gold Medal given that year, awarded for its plate and sheet iron. The clang and throb of the works was the heartbeat of the village and never stopped from Monday to Friday. A great disadvantage of living in Wilden House was that like all the houses near to the works, it suffered constant fallout of large, black smuts. Being the man he was, Alfred felt he must share his workers' tribulations and live with the smuts rather than move further away. He did not look for gratitude for the school, church, or any other largesse. He saw it all as his duty to his workers and their families.

Charles Crowther and his siblings grew up in this sheltered village environment with its patriarchal, deeply caring employer who looked after his workforce well but demanded good behaviour from all both at work and in their own time. Though the work was heavy and dirty, men went to work in a clean shirt each morning. Alfred was, at the same time, very mindful of the needs of his workforce. On one occasion a virtuous busybody asked why the King of Prussia (later Wilden Inn) was open from early morning till late at night. The reply was that Alfred willed it so because his men needed to replace the many pints of sweat which they shed every day in his employment! Little wonder that men like Charles were bound up in a tradition of service, hard work, church attendance and, perhaps even more than devotion to nation, a devotion to the county of Worcestershire. Stanley's cousin, Rudyard Kipling (who was Louisa Baldwin's godson as well as nephew), seems to have spent much holiday time at Wilden House, as did a collection of other Baldwin cousins and the Crowther boys. Stanley, Rudyard and their cousins did whatever it was that boys did in school holidays then. My great-aunt, Alice (Charles' older sister), was heard to say that 'Master Ruddy' was a young devil for enraging William with cheeky verses scribbled on the coach house wallpaper. My father, ever practical, always said it was a great pity someone did not have the wit to salvage some of the wallpaper with its unpublished Kipling!

One story which my father told me many times concerned a fledgling white owl which the Crowther boys found and took home to nurse and then tame. From across the lane, the Baldwin cousins coveted the owl and bribes were offered. Nothing would persuade the Crowthers to part with it. Many years later, Stanley Baldwin told my father that the owl came to represent for him the precious things in life which money cannot buy, and on which one cannot put a price. When Stanley became the first Earl Baldwin and acquired a coat of arms, it contained owls. Some time later Wilden School adopted a uniform badge with owls in it, now affectionately known locally as 'the Wilden Owls'.

This then was Charles' Wilden. It was also Stanley's beloved place to come home to in school holidays, and a Mecca for his cousins. Who knows how much their boyhood attitudes influenced each other and rubbed off on the other youngsters growing up in Wilden? But the facts are that in 1914, Charles, at the age of forty-two with four small children and a pregnant wife, would be the first Wilden man to volunteer to fight, Stanley would devote his life to public service and Rudyard would write patriotic verse to stir the heart and soul. A distant relative of mine, whose father spent a considerable amount of time with Stanley Baldwin, believed, in common with many who knew him, that Rudyard wrote his poem 'If' with Stanley in mind. It also seems very appropriate for my grandfather and his fellow volunteers; patriotic fervour and sense of duty abounded, and by the beginning of 1916 the relatively small village of Wilden, with less than 100 households, had over fifty men on active service.

Charles was not academically inclined, unlike his sister, Alice, who became a headmistress. He went to work for Alfred in the ironworks. In 1901, at the age of thirty, he married Dora Kate Mayall. They met as a result of football. Dora Kate, her older sister Laura, and their brothers were all involved with the Hoobrook Olympic Football Club. The Mayalls ran the Viaduct Inn, which nestled in the lee of the new Kidderminster Railway Viaduct, on the Wilden side of Kidderminster. The stunning blue-brick viaduct, replacing an earlier wooden Brunel one, had been built between 1883 and 1885 by the Earl of Dudley with Dora Kate's maternal uncle, Bill Tipper, as Clerk of Works. The football club was run from the Viaduct Inn, and both Mayalls and Tippers were involved with the running, coaching and playing. The Crowther boys were part of the scene, as was a young man by the name of William Bourne.

Dora Kate's sister, Laura (five years her senior), married William Bourne in 1891, and ten years later Dora Kate married Charles Crowther. Both couples settled down in Wilden, near to each other, just across the lane from the works. After Charles' death, William Bourne became a father-figure for Charles' elder son, Wilfred. William was known as Shammy because he was devoted to shamrock; he always kept a pot of it on his kitchen window sill, and on the day he died his current plant keeled over and could not be revived. In the lovely photograph of Shammy and Laura taken on the day of their golden wedding anniversary, he is sporting a bunch of shamrock in his buttonhole. (By a curious coincidence 'shammy' was the nickname for one of the jobs in the works, but not his). William junior, one of the younger sons of Shammy and Laura, and the same age as Wilfred, would be not just Wilfred's cousin, but his great friend. They would work together at the works all their lives, play cricket and football together and share the ups and downs of Wilden Home Guard during the Second World War. (To my father's chagrin, his job was a Reserved Occupation. Master rollers could not be spared to fight.

There was a fourteen-year gap between Arthur, oldest child of Shammy and Laura, and Wilfred. Dora Kate and Charles were married ten years after Shammy and Laura, and sadly lost their first three children in infancy. The maturity of older cousins nearby gave added stability to the lives of Charles' small children after his death. In fact, Arthur Bourne was godfather to Charles' youngest child, Louisa, born after his last leave. Later on, a twenty-one-year-old Wilfred would save Shammy's youngest son, Harry, from drowning in Wilden Pool and be awarded the Royal Humane Society's Certificate for Bravery.

As a small child, Wilfred so adored and shadowed his father that he was known to the village as 'Little Tim' after Dickens' Tiny Tim. Apart from his sisters, aunts and mother, Wilfred was known to everyone as Tim for his whole life, even though he grew to 6ft 3in and seventeen stone, with a thumb-tip to little-finger-tip measurement of 13½in. I for my part have been known to many as Timsann!

William Crowther in 1868, at
the time of his marriage to Eliza
Lippett. This is taken from a tiny,
painted miniature in a locket
which belonged to Eliza. The
likeness to two of his children,
Susan and Phillip, is unmistakable.
A recently discovered photograph
of William taken many years later is
recognisable as the same man.

Eliza Lippett around 1868,
probably at the time of her
marriage to William Crowther.
Both of them had been in Alfred
Baldwin's employ for two years by
then and were married from his
house in Bewdley.

Alfred Baldwin, probably during the 1870s.

Louisa Baldwin in 1870, when Stanley was three.

This is almost certainly William Crowther at the coach house in 1900, though it is not verified. The child is probably Phillip Crowther's little daughter, Kathleen, William's first grandchild. Phillip was coachman at Brockencote House in Chaddesley Corbett. This is one of a large group of photographs taken on glass negatives by Harry in 1900 before he left for the Boer War.

Wilden House, showing its two wings at right angles, one coming right down to the lane.

Wilden House staff in 1900, photographed by Harry. The glass plates were developed nearly sixty years later by a young Ray Carpenter. The fine hats were in honour of a day out for the ladies. They travelled in a large wagon which set off, presumably, as soon as they had posed for the photograph.

More Wilden House staff, photographed by Harry at the same time as the day out.

Opposite Wilden Church, photographed from the churchyard in the late 1950s.

Chapter Two

Why?

Charles and Dora Kate were married in Alfred's church in 1901, with the service conducted by William Cory. That was the year of Edward VII's accession. Their prospects looked good. He had a well-paid, highly-skilled job working for a benevolent employer who counted Charles' father, William, as a dear friend as well as an employee. Charles and his fellow master rollers, who were immensely skilled, wore bowler hats to walk to work as a mark of distinction. One of my cousins can remember his grandfather strutting his stuff to work in the prestigious headgear.

The newlyweds moved into one of the new 'Coronation Cottages' built by Dora Kate's uncle, Bill Tipper, at Brookside, across the lane from the works. To celebrate their marriage they borrowed a farm cart and had a day's outing to Martley, some miles away across the Severn, where they visited Charles' uncle and aunt who farmed land for a local landowner. The aunt was considered to be psychic and could understand communication between rooks. On their arrival she said the rooks, which were making a chaotic noise, were upset because there had just been a death. Thereupon the squire's steward arrived to fetch help for his master, who had fallen off his horse and broken his neck; he later proved to be dead! The aunt's sister understood bee language and, via the bees, accurately foretold several national calamities, including the Tay Bridge disaster in December 1879, though I do not think she actually named the bridge! Apparently my great-grandfather, William, a down-to-earth man, explained all this weird 'carry-on' as the unfortunate result of our being descended from the seventh son of a seventh son. This pronouncement was always accompanied by a deep, resigned sigh. (Modern research suggests that country families living close to the land for centuries may be able to detect much from creatures, such as bees and rooks, which operate in colonies.)

For as far back as we have traced family records, the Crowther family moved through a circle of small villages which were centred around Witley Court, a great and affluent house which offered much agricultural work, demand for maids of all sorts, and many other ancillary services. When a medicinal spring was discovered in 1839, nearby Tenbury Wells became a spa town. The road through Kidderminster to North Wales was a main coaching route from London and passed close to Tenbury Wells. Soon the rich, the famous and the royal sought invitations to Witley Court which, being near the new spa, was conveniently situated for taking the waters. Those who worked in that area saw many colourful comings and goings of high society, including Edward VII.

The close interdependence of local workers and great landowners not only coloured opinion, but bred great loyalty, particularly in north-west Worcestershire and on into Herefordshire, where life was comfortable and work was plentiful. There was a long history of loyalty to the throne. During the Civil War in the mid-seventeenth century, Worcestershire was one great battlefield and one can safely assume that the people who served the great landowners were Royalist. Charles' mother, Eliza, had a forbear joyously named Brilliana Thomas, in tribute to Lady Brilliana Harvey, a Civil War heroine who was a distant ancestor.

Charles' parents, William and Eliza, had first met Alfred Baldwin in 1863-64; they were working near William's family home which was in the village of Shrawley, only a few miles from Bewdley, Stourport and Wilden, where the Baldwin family had many business interests. Their romance was blossoming just as they met Alfred. It would seem that there was no real lack of money in William's family; he had been at school into his teens and his eldest sister never worked. Even after William's father and older brother both died prematurely, his mother and sister lived comfortably while bringing up one of William's nephews. Eliza's parents were farmers across the border in Herefordshire; they owned a house called Bigfield Green, which sat in four acres of land. As one would say in Worcestershire, they both had a bit of something about them! When they went to work for Alfred, living with him in his Bewdley house, being married from there, and then moving to Wilden with him, they embarked upon a lifetime of unswerving loyalty and hard work. Their reward was a deep and lasting friendship, and this, coupled with respect and a deep sense of gratitude, greatly influenced their young family as they grew up. It partly explains Charles' view of service to king, country, and to those in authority.

Life was so much more uncertain then, with high infant mortality and huge medical advances still to come, which we now take for granted. Much sorrow came to Charles and Dora Kate during the early years of marriage, despite all the advantages of a good job, a loving, large family on both sides, and the unique background of life in Wilden. Their fourth child, Wilfred, was the first of their children to survive infancy. I have some touching notes from Louisa Baldwin to Dora Kate as each new tragedy occurred.

During this time, Alfred Baldwin died very suddenly in 1908, leaving his wife, Louisa, and her sister, Edith, on their own at Wilden House. Edith was younger than Louisa, and never married. Louisa was not strong, and was particularly frail when Stanley was young. Edith came to live at Wilden House to help Louisa cope with the growing boy, and then simply stayed. 1913 brought news from Canada that Frank, youngest of all Charles' siblings, had died at the age of thirty-three. He had settled over there not long before, working as a successful photographer. Everything began to look different. The old order was changing, and the Baldwins looked to the future by purchasing motor cars for the works, including a splendid Sunbeam with the registration number BA 35. Coachman William was in fact pushing seventy, and was possibly relieved, but it was the end of an era, though he stayed officially in Louisa's employ. Finally, there was the worry of Harry, another of Charles' younger brothers. He was both physically and emotionally damaged after a spell in the Boer War with the Worcestershire Volunteers. A clutch of medals was no consolation for the loss of the old Harry.

Of Charles' siblings, Harry and Frank were the artistic ones; they were also very young and headstrong. Headmistress Alice was caring and organising, but she had a career and many other interests. She played the piano well, and began teaching me when I was three. She was also a walking encyclopaedia of British flora. She and Charles were very close, and he always looked to her for advice. The two brothers between Charles and Harry had long since married and left home. It was gentle, caring Charles who provided physical and emotional support for his parents, who were ageing fast and worried about Harry, and by 1913 were mourning Frank. Susie, born between Harry and Frank, was brought up to be a lady. She lived to be ninety-three and never mastered the basics of cooking and other household skills. Right to the end, neighbours as old as she would 'pop round' with homemade suet puddings and egg custards to sustain her.

Harry and Frank were both photographic buffs. Frank had trained as a carpet designer, but then became a professional photographer. Harry was an enthusiastic and talented amateur. I have some of Harry's wonderful glass negatives of Baldwin children, Baldwin staff, Wilden ladies in fine hats, William in his garden, Charles in the famous bowler hat, and a glorious one of himself taken through the keyhole of his garden shed while very drunk! These date from 1900 to 1905. Harry's job was as bookkeeper at the Anglo-American Enamel Works a mile away in Stourport. His copperplate writing and beautifully formed numbers were famous throughout the county. He loved to make and use quill pens; I use the old family oak bureau almost every day and cannot help but smile at the mess he made of the writing surface as he sharpened his quills. The bureau dates from 1640, so I daresay many more Crowthers than Harry sliced away on it over the centuries since we acquired it.

When in 1900, aged twenty-two, Harry volunteered for the Boer War, apparently on a whim, he was carried shoulder-high to the railway station at Stourport and sent off to the sound of ringing cheers. He came back seriously wounded and with a changed personality. However, the memory of it had the whiff of adventure about it, even twelve years later in 1914. Harry's enthusiastic volunteering and the carnival atmosphere of his send-off give us more insight as to why Charles should, at the age of forty-two, cheerfully set off to right the world, leaving behind a pregnant wife, four small children aged one to eight, and ageing parents. All his life my father vividly remembered the day Charles volunteered. He was in the kitchen with his mother, watching her cook the lunch when his father burst in, pink-faced and grinning from ear to ear. He shouted, 'Well, kid, I've done it, I've joined up!' She boxed his ears and yelled, 'You bloody fool!' But she never said anything disloyal after that one outburst. In a perverse way she and the family were proud of the fact that he was the first Wilden man to volunteer. He was also the first to die.

So what drove them? Yes, they were full of patriotic fervour, a sense of duty, and all the other community-centred feelings that abounded in the agricultural shires of

Frank Crowther was the youngest of all Charles' siblings. His high, stiff collar was the height of fashion from the late 1890s to 1903.

Middle England. Such men with good, well-paid jobs did not need to seek the king's shilling. But they had lived very restricted, sheltered lives in the womb-like security of villages like Wilden. Fired with the excitement of going outside Worcestershire, never mind abroad, it must have seemed like a good adventure. Ingenuousness and ignorance of the wider picture led men like Charles to think they would bustle off abroad and sort out the enemy and Europe, and be home in time to celebrate both victory and Christmas. It is touching to observe in Charles' letters home how it finally dawns on him that it is going to be 'a long job'. In the early letters during the muster of the British Mediterranean Expeditionary Force, Charles writes chirpily of the prospect of a three-week sea voyage to the Mediterranean… this was a man who had seen the sea for the first time earlier that year, and only the Channel at that! Everything was interesting and new.

Charles Crowther in 1901, at the time of his marriage to Dora Kate Mayall. The wedding was in Wilden Church, with Harry Cory officiating.

Dora Kate Mayall in 1901, just before her marriage to Charles Crowther.

Harry Crowther volunteered for the Boer War in 1900; he was one of ten local Volunteers chosen to go to South Africa for special duties (bandsman and stretcher-bearer), with the 1st Volunteer Battalion of the Worcestershire Regiment. The wings on the shoulders of his uniform denote bandsman.

The Volunteers' camp.

These men from the 1st Worcs Volunteer Regiment are in the old bottle-green uniform worn by the Volunteers until 1908, when they became the Territorials and acquired a new uniform.

All four Volunteers' camp photographs were taken with Harry's camera.

Alfred Baldwin's funeral at Wilden in 1908, taken from behind the church.

Looking back at the funeral of Alfred Baldwin, from the field across the road. The white building on the hill is the vicarage.

Kidderminster Viaduct in 1905. The Mayalls' Viaduct Inn was just beyond the right of the photograph.

Hoobrook Olympic Football Team in 1915. Syd Mayall is second from left in the third row, Bill Tipper junior is on the far left of the second row and Jack Tipper is on the far right of the second row.

Chapter Three

France

When Charles volunteered in the early autumn of 1914, my grandmother was at first livid, but ever afterwards was staunchly loyal and supportive. He had a short spell in the Volunteers; by then they had had a change of uniform and were renamed the Territorials, but the old, affectionate name of Volunteers stuck. He was soon assigned to the 1st Worcestershire, an infantry battalion, and was sent to France to join them, disembarking on 19 March 1915. He was seriously wounded fairly soon after arriving, and was shipped home to a military hospital in Manchester.

There are no surviving letters from the French episode, but my father always remembered a letter he had received from Charles which made a big impression on a little boy of eight. Apparently Charles' battalion were near to a convent; he wrote that when there was fighting, the nuns came during the night with carts and took away the wounded. Charles wrote that as they passed, a scent of violets would drift down into the trenches. The small boy took this as some sort of miraculous sign of holiness. However, I was recently told that there is a herb in that part of France which, when crushed by feet, gives off a scent very like violets. Perhaps both explanations are valid.

Early in 1915 the 1st Worcestershire were in Artois in advance of the main spring offensive which attempted to break the German front line south of Ypres. Here, the German salient, a bulge westwards in their front line, curved back eastwards near Neuve Chappelle. They fought in the Battle of Neuve Chappelle from 10-13 March and did indeed break the German line, but the results of the success were quickly lost. Charles sailed to join the 1st Worcestershire as part of a draft of two officers and 137 other ranks sent to strengthen them. Events rolled onwards to the follow-up battle at Aubers Ridge on 9 May. Looking at the records of the 1st Worcestershire in France in April and May 1915, it is clear that Charles must have fought and been wounded at Aubers Ridge. After that he was soon back in England, before the 1st fought another battle, though his name is not on the list of Worcestershire wounded. Aubers Ridge has been described as an unmitigated disaster and one of the worst days in British Army history. The 1st Worcestershire's records note that two battalions, the

Sherwood Foresters and the 2nd East Lancashire, became hopelessly intermixed and that the 1st Worcestershire were unable to get through the melee to their assigned positions. As German shells crashed onto this confusion and rifle and machine-gun fire raked all open ground, a fallen Worcester man could easily find himself on the wrong list of casualties. This is the best scenario I can come up with; certainly it fits the time frame, for Charles was shipped home and put in hospital for two or three weeks, given a short home leave, and promptly re-assigned to the 5th Worcestershire before July. Brigade records tell of the many wounded being gathered up and taken to relative safety, presumably without sorting into regiments. I suspect that many more men failed to appear on the appropriate lists of wounded, or even on a list at all. Since his service record no longer exists, we shall never know for sure.

No one at home in Wilden ever said much about my grandfather's exploits in France. I suspect the main reason was that Gallipoli and his death made the French episode seem irrelevant to his loved ones. When Charles sailed for France, Dora Kate was four months pregnant, and had four very young children to cope with; she was over forty and this would be her eighth child. Betty was twenty months old, Arthur was four, Marjorie was just seven, and Wilfred was almost nine. And while Dora Kate reeled from the enormity of it all, nearby, Laura and Shammy were trying to come to terms with the fact that their oldest son, Arthur, would soon enlist. After leaving the Manchester hospital and visiting home, Charles was immediately back with the Army and settling into quarters on the South Coast, in the Plymouth area.

Charles was assigned to the 5th Worcestershire, a reserve battalion. A reserve battalion absorbed injured and over-age men, and Charles was both. Such battalions provided workers to load supplies in depots, docks, on hospital ships and so on, here or anywhere in the war arena. In his early letters from Plymouth, Charles was naively enthusiastic about all the new experiences and the prospect of a possible trip abroad to somewhere rather exotic, such as Malta. Men like Charles seem to have been unaware of the wider plan for the men assigned to the Plymouth area. They only fully realised where they were going when they were actually on board ship and en route.

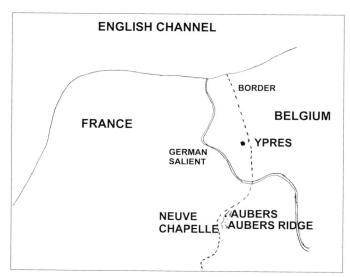

A map of Artois in Spring 1915, from Ypres down to Neuve Chappelle and Aubers Ridge, showing the German salient.

Chapter Four

Devon

Charles arrived in the Plymouth area at the beginning of July 1915, following his spell in the Manchester hospital and re-assignment to the 5th Worcestershire, a reserve battalion, stationed in Devon at the time. In the nineteenth century, Palmerston had built defensive forts around major naval installations on the South Coast. These had now been called into use both for strategic purposes and to muster men for the British Mediterranean Expeditionary Force. Charles went first to Picklecombe Fort, with views for miles out to sea. The place was full of vivid contrasts for him. It was a beautiful spot, but Charles and his fellows were there to guard the Plymouth Sound, as well as preparing to go abroad. There was a battery of heavy artillery and a great mass of floodlights. Badly damaged ships limped in, and every vessel in and out was checked. Charles was aware that it was a dangerous place to be, but he was enchanted by the spectacle and the new experiences.

After eight days he was moved on to nearby Fort Tregantle. He worked in the cookhouse as well as doing guard duties, and had a good idea of the kind of support work the 5th Worcestershire would eventually be asked to do. While he knew men were being moved on all the time, he did not know that members of the British Mediterranean Expeditionary Force had been going out from the South Coast in waves since early in the year.

Despite buzzing with enthusiasm for the exciting new experiences, Charles had both financial and domestic worries. His pay was always late and always less than it should have been (Not the regiment's fault!). Not only did he often not have enough money to meet friends for a drink, but he did not have enough for postage as he began to try to send all his personal belongings home. Things were also less than perfect at home; Dora Kate's baby was due any day. Despite the possible problems with an eighth child at her age, there would be little help for her because two of Charles' brothers were living away from Wilden, another was dead, and his two sisters, one of whom was a busy teacher, were tied up caring for brother Harry and his little family, who were not coping well. Alice and Susie had in fact left their cottage in Hartlebury in order to move in with Harry, his wife and young daughter, Mollie, who was seven, the same age as Marjorie. Meanwhile, Charles' parents were in their seventies with no one to keep an eye on them except Louisa Baldwin, by whom William was still officially employed even though the coach was now more or less unused. Most Wilden families were by now caught up in their own nightmares, Dora Kate's eldest nephew, Arthur Bourne, was old enough to fight, and Laura and Shammy were 'near mad' about that.

Dora Kate gave birth to her baby on 9 August and named her Louisa for Mrs Baldwin, and Mary for the Queen. Charles liked the names. By the end of August he was passed fit for active service, but was not given any idea of where he might be sent. His battalion were now standing by. He was still short of money for posting his belongings back to Wilden, and worse still, had no money with which to buy baby Louisa a small gift. Problems with pay were a constant thorn in the flesh.

In mid-September Charles had another medical. amd along with the other men who passed, he was kitted out and given the order to stand to. It was impossible to find time to write to anyone other than his wife, and he felt guilty that his mother would not get the longed-for letter from him. After six days of standing to, the men were getting edgy and restless; suddenly they were told they would be sailing in four days' time. Charles had been delighted to hear that young Arthur Bourne had stood as godfather when baby Louisa was christened; it was a small thing, but choosing names, godparents and generally arranging a christening were part of a swift learning curve for Dora Kate. She was now on her own and was going to have to make all family decisions by herself.

Things now began to move swiftly and the sailing date was brought forward by two days. Charles was convinced that the war could not go on for long, and told his wife not to worry. He was looking forward to a nice three-week voyage and an interesting job on Malta. From his references to Malta and the Dardanelles, it is clear that Charles had no idea where or what the Dardanelles was; he seems to have thought that it and Malta were connected in some way. A week later he wrote home on an official blue postcard; these appear to have been handed out at certain points for all the men to send a short message home. He wrote jauntily about being 'on the briny somewhere off Gib'. From then on the men were very limited as to what information they could send home; place names were forbidden, for instance,. Also, it is very clear that the men were given hardly any information at all. From leaving Plymouth to arriving fatally wounded on Malta ten weeks later, Charles did not see a newspaper, receive any mail or glean any idea of what was going on anywhere in Europe.

Two days after sending the jaunty postcard, Charles wrote home from the ship HMS *Majestic* on 1 October. The letter had been censored. There had been a major shift in his situation; he had sailed from Devon as a member of the 5th Battalion (reserve), but he was now attached to the 9th Battalion (replacement), of the 13th Division in the 39th Brigade of the British Mediterranean Expeditionary Force. For the first time he wrote 9th Worcs on his letter. He was not going to Malta; they were heading for the Dardanelles and Gallipoli (though the men were not allowed to mention names), and what had promised to be a fascinating voyage could not be a pleasure because of what the men now knew lay ahead of them. Clinging to ties with home, Charles began a daily ritual of looking at photographs of Arthur, Marjorie and Wilfred, which he carried with him. (Sadly, there had not been a photograph of Betty to hand when he left home. Though it is certain that Dora Kate sent one later, as we now know, Charles did not receive any mail until the next January when he was on Malta.)

After nineteen days, the *Majestic* arrived in Suvla Bay and the men were kept on the overcrowded ship for three days in the harbour. It must have been the stuff of nightmares to be absorbed into the noise and mayhem of the harbour which was crammed with every sort of vessel, including the British Navy ships which were constantly bombarding the Turkish positions on the hillside above the bay. So this was Gallipoli!

William Crowther in late middle age, around 1910. The original photograph in Earl Baldwin's collection has a handwritten caption which reads, 'he was for 57 years in the service of Mr and Mrs Alfred Baldwin and was a valued friend in the family'.

Alice Crowther in her twenties, around 1892; the photograph is from a small Christmas card, which reads 'Seasonal Greetings'.

Susan Crowther, probably taken for her twenty-first birthday in 1900

Chapter Five

Gallipoli

During September, while Charles was preparing to leave Plymouth, the 9th Worcestershire, his new battalion, were in the front line in Gallipoli around Sulajik. They formed part of the main line of defence across the low-lying scrubland facing the Anafarta Hills; it was rough and fairly open terrain. They were about one mile south of the land held by the 4th Worcestershire. Constant shellfire and busy Turkish snipers were the order of the day rather than concerted military action. Snipers were the cause of most losses and incessant work was needed to keep the trenches relatively well-protected and concealed with parapets, which were mounds of earth and stone built along the front of the trenches facing the enemy. Wiring parties went out under the cover of darkness, attempting to impede the enemy advance across no man's land towards the British trenches. The Turks, holed up in the hills, were helped by perfect weather and bright moonlight as they raked the low ground where the 9th Worcestershire were.

Situated within modern-day Turkey, the Dardanelles is part of a stretch of water separating Europe from Asia. The Gallipoli Peninsular forms its western shoreline. In ancient times the Dardanelles was known as the Hellespont. Its entrance from the Mediterranean Sea is two miles in width, widening out to five miles. It narrows to a mile and a half before reaching the Narrows, where the two land masses are only three-quarters of a mile apart. The Dardanelles then leads into the Sea of Marmora and up to Istanbul with its access to the Black Sea via another narrow channel, the Bosphorus. The Dardanelles has been of strategic importance since King Xerxes of ancient Persia crossed the Narrows to invade Greece. When Winston Churchill gained Cabinet permission for the 1915 Gallipoli campaign, he hoped to knock Turkey out of the war and free up the vital sea route for the Allies, particularly Russia.

It is doubtful whether Charles ever fully understood what the Dardanelles was, or why he was fighting Turks in that part of the world. In his letter of 15 September, written before sailing, Charles had confused the Dardanelles with Malta, and he had no chance to get a real grasp of the geography of the place because after being cooped up in the harbour on the ship for three days, the men went ashore at night and were marched under heavy fire straight to the trenches. Charles sent news of his arrival in the trenches on a stark blue postcard, written whilst shells were flying overhead. That was 11 October. During the last four days of September, the 9th Worcestershire had had several skirmishes in which a small number of them successfully saw off large numbers of Turks; the Divisional Commander, General Maude, was very appreciative of these exploits because the troops' morale was low. The men were depressed, suspicious of mismanagement, and there were other issues of war such as the sinking of mail and supply vessels by enemy submarines. The troops' main interests were always mail and eatables.

It was difficult to write informative letters to loved ones desperate for news; it was forbidden to send any real information home, either geographical or military. In addition, Charles was aware that his wife, parents, sisters and children would all read and re-read his letters. He managed to give them a very real sense of what his life was like, without burdening them with the horror; but it was always there, just below the surface in his letters. A few days after arriving, Charles began to realise that they would be there for a long time. Despite the constant British Naval bombardment day and night over the heads of the soldiers, there was no sign of an advance and it was unsettling that the Turks were virtually invisible and therefore difficult to pinpoint from the ground below. Life in general was very uncomfortable and the three main problems were proving to be a lot of flies in the heat of day, bitterly cold nights and insufficient water. Even so, Charles still retained his interest and curiosity in all things new; he was touchingly intrigued to find himself using water from a well such as he had seen in Bible illustrations. On the subject of flies, there is a telling extract from a young Worcestershire soldier's journal in which he writes that a major problem with the swarming flies was that one inevitably acquired small cuts and grazes to the hands which normally would barely be noticed. After some horrendous incidents due to the ever-constant flies, many soldiers kept their hands permanently bandaged to avoid both damage and infestation. This applied equally to trenches and docks.

Charles was not a man to bemoan his lot, but the lack of any news from home was adding to his sense of isolation in a once beautiful landscape where there was not a single building left standing. The children had had whooping cough in September; in those days it could be a dangerous illness, and he had no idea of how they were now. He had not seen the new baby, and did not know whether Dora Kate was fully fit and strong again. He was anxious for both national and domestic news, for the promise of a Christmas cake, and for a beer.

By the end of October it was three months since Charles had last seen his family. On a personal level, life was spartan; provisions were basic, brought up from the harbour at night under heavy fire. Plenty of tobacco was distributed, but Charles was fantasising about a taste of cheese and Shammy's home brew. Almost every time Charles wrote home, he said that he hoped Wilfred was being a good boy and helping his mother. Charles would never know just how much his young son was doing. He was helping his uncle, Sidney Mayall, in the Viaduct Inn, and earning money doing all manner of other jobs. And he always kept a close eye on his mother.

Matters limped on into November. Pleasant autumn began to turn into stormy winter. There was not much activity, but much loss of life from rifle and shell. Monotony was the insidious enemy; for days on end there was no fresh food and sickness was rife in the trenches. All battalions were seriously under strength, and there was a feeling of instability as officers fell or were recalled and had to be replaced. The men were exhausted; when they came off the front line to have a day or two in the rest trenches they had to go out at night on wiring duty. There was no respite. At the beginning of November a great many Territorials arrived in Gallipoli. Charles wrote home saying how much they would be needed to boost numbers if a move was to be made; he did not add the obvious, that they were needed anyway as replacements for the fallen. A church service was held in the Worcestershire trenches, to the accompaniment of constant shellfire, though luckily no one was hit. Charles had still not had a single letter or card, but he was philosophical, never doubting that his loved ones were writing to him. Meanwhile, constant trench digging went on as they tried to get nearer to the Turks. By the second week of November they had still not moved position; the days remained hot, but the nights were even colder than before. Proper sleep was impossible in the trenches, but in any case many nights were taken up with wiring parties and more digging. Charles thought longingly of a comfortable bed, and imagined the increasing excitement of his small children as Christmas approached.

It was vital to hang on to positive images as the monotony and hard labour bit into mental as well as physical reserves. They were taking very heavy fire, and no progress was being made. In what would prove to be his last letter from Gallipoli, Charles made a very accurate assessment of the situation. He said that the naval bombardment, though heavy, could not succeed on its own. Some of the enemy would have to be taken out by the ground forces. He wrote simply, 'It will have to be done.' By now it had begun to rain; and it persisted unremittingly in torrents for the next two weeks. A few days after writing his last Gallipoli letter, Charles went down with a severe bout of dysentery and had to go into the field hospital for a week. While he was there, the result of two weeks of non-stop rain finally flooded the trenches on 26 November. A great bank of cloud unleashed a tremendous thunderstorm. The trenches filled rapidly, their protective parapets crumbling. 4½in of rain fell in an hour and a half. Rifles and ammunition were swept away; many men drowned, while others were clinging to life, up to their necks in very cold water. The 9th Worcestershire worked tirelessly to empty the trenches and rebuild the parapets, and some order was restored. General Maude applauded the efforts of the 9th and the 39th Brigade to which they belonged, but the next day it continued to rain; nothing could be dried, and fires would not light. The Turks were in a similar plight, and huddles of men from both sides sat about, too wretched for hostility. A large number of Turks surrendered at this point. Meanwhile, trench foot was breaking out

By 28 November there was great suffering all along the Worcestershire line. The colonel worked forty-eight hours without sleep; his adjutant 'went through the lines giving hot tea and Bovril to men who were frozen in, and never rested once in four days, rushing about doing everybody's work' (extract taken from a private soldier's letter). General Maude battled the weather to have a look for him, and sent up rum and extra fuel (though it was too wet to light). The battalion diary records that the enemy seemed totally demoralised and large numbers were killed as they wandered about aimlessly across open ground.

The weather had one more diabolical trick to play. Overnight the temperature plummeted, rain turned to snow and everything froze, particularly the wet and miserable troops. A sentry was found frozen to death at his post, and several small groups, huddled together, died of exposure as they failed to find any cover. Frostbite was now another debilitating problem. Next morning, Monday 29 November, Charles, still suffering from dysentery, was released from hospital and returned to the front line. Only those who were totally debilitated and unable to stand could now be classed as sick. Charles was promptly sent out on a wiring party and in a short space of time was seriously wounded. A rifle bullet lodged in his shoulder, followed by shrapnel which went through his shoulder and travelled down into his stomach, damaging a lung on the way. He still had dysentery, and now he also had frostbite. The catastrophic weather was the catalyst that triggered the end of the campaign in Gallipoli, and the beginning of the evacuation of the British. A young subaltern of the 9th wrote in his journal:

Nov 27th Weather conditions simply appalling.

Nov 28th I am given charge of 100 men unfit for work. My orders are to take them back to some support trenches… the water is so deep that we have to get out and walk along the top… two men in each other's embrace are found frozen to death. They had tried to get warmth of each other's body… We get to the support trench, which is worse than the front line… and work to improve the trench… it freezes hard… later snow and frost…

Nov 29th Rheumatism and sore feet, I hobble along… attend to the sick and dying… boil up quantities of hot tea and rum.

Nov 30th All my NCOs have left, really ill… thirty of my hundred men left, the others either carried back or dead… no firing today, rifles won't work.

Dec 1st I receive orders to return to the front line with my party… accordingly I set out… I only get ten men back to the line.

The Worcestershire Regimental Medical Officer, Lieutenant Galbraith, was the only doctor left in the whole 39th Brigade; he did his best in an impossible situation. Help for Charles and many others was a long time in coming. In view of the weather conditions and his dreadful wounds, it almost passes belief that he clung to life at all. Charles' wait for hospital treatment was agonising; for the first day or two, there was simply nowhere to lie down. However, the next day, 30 November, the weather brightened and some degree of drying out was possible. The major problem of rescue had been caused by the great thunderstorm of 29 November which interrupted communications, which meant that the hospital ships could not come near land and there was only very limited accommodation in the field hospital. For several days injured men were considered to be better off with their division.

The whole situation was disastrous and a decision to begin the withdrawal from Gallipoli was made. Finally, on Saturday 4 December, four days after being wounded, Charles was taken down to the harbour and put on a ship for Malta. He was taken to the Royal Naval Hospital at Bighi, high on the cliffs above the fishing village of Kalkara, looking out to sea over Valletta. Meanwhile, the 9th Worcestershire had the dubious honour of being selected to stay to the very end to oversee the conclusion to the British action in Gallipoli.

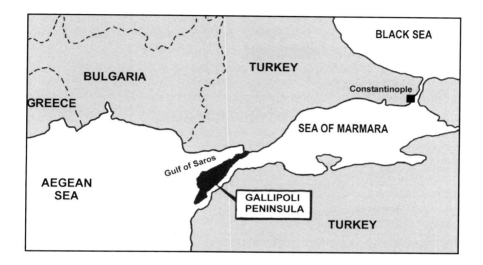

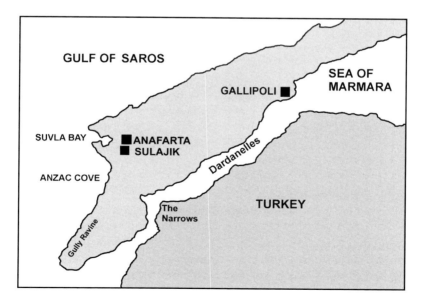

The 4th and 9th Worcestershires, as part of the 13th Division of the 39th Brigade, were dug in near Suvla Bay.

Wilfred and Marjorie in 1914, aged eight and six, photographed specially for Charles. He carried this with him throughout his time in the Army, and had a nightly ritual in Gallipoli of 'having a look at them'. The photographer had been late arriving at the house, by which time they and their Sunday best were filthy; Dora Kate had to put them into their clean school clothes and was not pleased.

Transport of the 4th Worcestershire at Gully Ravine. (Courtesy of the Worcestershire Regiment Museum Trust)

A periscope in use over the
forward parapet of one of
the Worcestershire trenches.
(Courtesy of the Worcestershire
Regiment Museum Trust)

Officer and soldier of the 4th
Worcestershire, in their trench.
(Courtesy of the Worcestershire
Regiment Museum Trust)

49

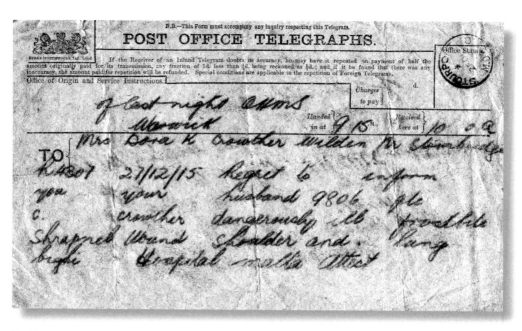

The official Post Office telegraph which arrived two days after Christmas 1915, a month after Charles was wounded.

This British Red Cross letter gave Dora Kate a very brief period of hope.

Chapter Six

Malta

While Charles was in the trenches, yearning for news of home, his loved ones had kept faith. Dora Kate, Alice, the children, friends and Louisa Baldwin had all written many times; gifts had been sent, including a Christmas pudding from Louisa. It is a mystery why nothing from the large volume of Wilden mail reached him before he arrived on Malta; but finally, three letters from Dora Kate, long delayed somewhere, caught up with her Charlie, though not until the turn of the year. By November she had begun to be less of a prisoner; in those days it was no easy matter to take a baby, a toddler, a naughty four-year-old ('a little hound') and two other children anywhere. She had finally walked all of them up to her parents-in-law at the coach house. Though they had been up and down to her, she had not visited them for six months. William and Eliza had had their house redecorated and she thought it very smart, but the cheeky Kipling limericks on the wallpaper were no more!

Life was difficult in Wilden, with rocketing prices, but Dora Kate could not even bring herself to wish for a pig like the ones Charles' father had fattened up for the winter unless Charlie was there to share it. Even basics such as soling and heeling a child's boots were a worry. Among the men left at home, work was not secure; Wilden Ironworks was on a much reduced schedule and gloom and financial insecurity hovered. Charles' children accepted that their dad was not coming home yet, and were anxious to know whether he would be hanging his stocking up for Christmas. During the weeks leading up to Christmas, Alice was a great support; her teaching experience stood her in good stead when dealing with Arthur, the mischievous 'little tinker'. She gave Dora Kate a whole day's respite by taking him to Kidderminster as a treat for his fifth birthday. In Charles' absence, and with her parents visibly slowing down, she took over the mantle of head of the family. Wilfred, Marjorie and Arthur, who all stayed locally as adults, repaid her care by 'keeping an eye on the aunties' until Alice died in 1950 and Susie in 1970.

Dora Kate was enchanted with baby Louisa, a real beauty. Like Arthur, she had flaming red hair. Wilfred always called her Redwing because as a child she ran everywhere with her mane of red hair streaming out behind her like a bird's wing. Virtually all the Crowthers had colouring ranging from blond to auburn. (We still have!) Dora Kate kept a light touch in her letters, and wrote wryly to her Charlie that she would see a lot more of him if he were in Wilden now that the pubs were being closed down. While she could smile at the thought, she was nevertheless feeling somewhat adrift. Everyone else had huge problems, not just she. Her sister Laura, who might have been a comfort, was almost prostrate at the thought of her son, Arthur, now enlisted, going off with the Welsh Fusiliers to fight in France any day. Dora Kate had not heard from Charlie since his last letter from Gallipoli on 15 November and was becoming uneasy. Meanwhile, Charles had arrived at the Royal Naval Hospital on Malta, There was a sort of giant dumb waiter which took the wounded up from the water to the hospital high on the cliffs. It also raised many other loads brought in by sea.

After four days at Bighi, Charles felt able to write home and tell them what had happened. In typical Charles fashion, he said it was not much and for them not to worry. Though playing down the seriousness of his injuries, Charles was now fully aware of how ill he was; and after months of shielding his wife from the horror of the war, he let down his guard by saying that if he did not receive his Christmas mail and gifts, then 'some other poor devil' would get them. At this point, Charles had not had a single letter from home since leaving Devon. A week later, and he still had not received a letter. He was very weak, the bullet was still lodged in his shoulder, and he was finally unable to bluff it out; he wrote a letter home in which he said 'Dear Wife' three times, and put twelve kisses at the bottom, two each for Dora Kate and the children; not his usual style.

A week later, on 26 December, Kathleen Fisher, one of the staff at Bighi, wrote to Dora Kate to add a personal touch to the official Army missive about Charles' injuries and situation which she knew would have arrived in Wilden by now. She promised to keep in touch and said that the hospital was doing all it possibly could for Charles. Although the official telegraph had reached Wilden promptly, his letters home from Bighi did not arrive until halfway through January. Dora Kate was hugely relieved to hear from her Charlie, but was very upset that none of the dozens of loving letters from Wilden had ever reached him, and neither had Mrs Baldwin's pudding. Christmas had been a non-event in Wilden; she and the children would have a special celebration with him when he finally came home. Through all the turmoil of war, the little family had to function on a practical basis, with problems such as a recently vaccinated baby, who was exceptionally 'cross'. Meanwhile, each child was planning a special outing with their father. A small glimmer of hope was offered by the Red Cross who wrote on 19 January to say that Charles was actually making satisfactory progress. Nurse Glover (Alice's friend) also wrote to report good progress, and said that Charles had been visited by the Governor of Malta, who had praised him.

By mid-January, Charles was in possession of three letters written by Dora Kate in November and early December. He then received another one, written after Christmas. At last he had a link with home. There was news of the children and young Arthur Bourne. There were Christmas gifts waiting to be sent on to Bighi, and things looked brighter. A fortnight later, on the last day of January, nothing much had yet happened. Though Charles had been x-rayed, they had not operated yet and the bullet had healed up in his shoulder. A certain passive acceptance can be felt in Charles' letter of 31 January. He wrote that so much mail has been lost at sea that it would not be wise to send any goods for the time being, though he would like news. He said he felt stronger, but writing was very painful. He had been touched to hear from the Vicar of Wilden, Mr Cory, and wanted his father to 'remember me to him'. Charles was slipping away; he had not had his operation because he was simply too weak for the doctors to risk it. Suddenly his condition deteriorated swiftly and the damage from his wounds, particularly to his lungs, made an operation vital, come what may. He was not strong enough, and died following the surgery on 2 February, four days before little Marjorie's eighth birthday.

Kathleen Fisher wrote to Wilden, clearly very sad at the loss of a man she had come to admire and like. Charles would be buried in the Royal Naval Cemetery at Bighi, with full military honours. She and other staff were endlessly kind; they organised flowers, photographed them, and those who could be spared went to the funeral. They did everything they could to make Dora Kate, Alice and Charles' parents feel involved as they struggled to cope with officialdom as well as grief. It transpires in letters written later on to Alice that Charles had discussed with the nurses the sorting of his affairs and the making of arrangements should the worst happen. The hospital staff had known of Charles' trust in her judgement, and were aware that Dora Kate would need all the help she could get. There was a certain sad inevitability about the brief but kind letter to Wilden from the Royal Naval Chaplain on Malta. He had buried Charles in the beautiful and well-tended Naval Cemetery at Bighi on 3 February.

A memorial service was held for Charles in Wilden Church on Sunday 13 February. Preaching to a packed church, Mr Cory took the Fifth Commandment as his text: 'Honour thy father and thy mother', and spoke of Charles' devotion to his family and love for his parents. He told the congregation, which contained many Baldwin employees, that nothing would have pleased the church's founder and benefactor more than to see such a brave man who had given his life for his country, being honoured on the very day when they were also commemorating the death of Alfred himself, some eight years earlier.

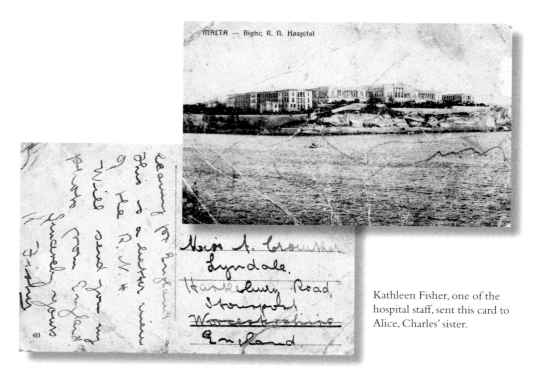

Kathleen Fisher, one of the hospital staff, sent this card to Alice, Charles' sister.

IN MEMORIAM.

Charles' grave after the funeral, with flowers from the hospital staff.

Opposite A mounted photograph of the Naval Cemetery, sent by hospital staff to Dora Kate.

The lift in Valletta harbour which took Charles up from the troop ship to the hospital high on the cliffs.

Charles' grave with flowers and a poppy cross taken by his granddaughter, Ann, in the 1990s, on her first visit just before 11 November.

English & French.

Russian.

Australian.

French.

Japanese.

New Zealand.

Union Jacks.

WILDEN.

Officers and Men on Service.

JANUARY, 1916.

Royal Navy.

Stoker G. Bentley, H.M.S. "Hercules."
Stoker A. Carradine, H.M.S. "Viking."
Pte. W. H. Tolley, R.M.L.I.
    H.M.S. "Venerable."

Army—Abroad.

Gnr. R. Bradley, R.F.A.
Pte. F. Harris, A.S.C.
   ,, T. Hurdman, 11th Worcs.
L. Corpl. B. W. Guest, Cyclist Corps.
Major A. Dore, 7th Worcs.
Sergt. W. Calcott,   ,,
Pte. G. Bourne   ,,
Pte. Harold Randle   ,,
Rifleman J. Pickering, Rifle Brigade
   ,,   W. H. Randle,   ,,
   ,,   F. Rosser   ,,
Pte. E. Pritchard, 10th Wors.
   ,, F. Powell, 7th Worcs.
   ,, W. Willetts ,,
   ,, A. Palmer, S.W. Borderers
   ,, F. Capewell ,,   ,,
   ,, L. Goodyear, 11th Worcs.
   ,, C. Crowther, 9th Worcs.
   ,, W. Everton, 3rd Worcs.
   ,, J. Pritchard, R. Warwicks
   ,, Albert Whitmore, 2nd Worcs.
   ,, Arthur Whitmore, 7th Worcs.
   ,, A. Pritchard, R.A M.C
   ,, W. H. Bough, 9th Worcs.
Gnr. H. Harper, R.F.A.
Q-Master Sergt. Bourne, Welsh Regt.

At Home.

Capt. P. Prince, K.S.L.I.
Rifleman G. Whitmore, Rifle Brigade.
Pte. J. Everton, N. Welsh Regiment.
   ,, C. Randle, 8th Worcs.

Pte. A. Jones, Wor. Yeomanry
   ,, F. Millward, 7th Worcs.
Driver F. Pickering, R.F.A.
Pte. W. J. Parry, 5th Worcs.
   ,, Thos. Roe, A.S.C.
Driver E. Randle, R.F.A.
Pte. J. Smith, 14th Worcs.
   ,, Geo. Jones, 50th Canadians.
   ,, Alfred Whitmore, 7th Worcs.
Driver Jas, South, R.F.A.
Pte. W. Goode, 14th Worcs.

Discharged, Wounded.
Pte. A. W. Carradine, 1st Worcs.

Wounded and Missing since July, 1915
Pte. C. Dudley, 3rd Worcs.

CHOIRMEN ON SERVICE.
Segt. W. Calcott, 7th Worcs.
Pte. P. Dorsett, R.A.M.C.
   ,, A. Pritchard, R.A.M.C.
Bandsman W. Evers, 14th Worcs.
       ,,   Harold Evers   ,,

FORMER MEMBERS OF CHOIR.
Bandmaster. Ken Glover, R. Welsh Rgt.
E. Osborne, H.M.S. "Ajax."
Sapper P. King, R.E.
Segt. R. Pritchard, R.G.A.
Segt. J. Pritchard, 5th Worcs.
Pte. Frank Dorsett, R.A.M.C.
Bandsman B. Evers, Grenadier Guards
Bandsman Harry Evers, Winnipeg L.I.
Pte. E. Harrison, Qs. Westminster Rfls.
   ,, W. Kimberley, Canadian E.F.

The *Wilden Almanac* of 1916, showing the list of Wilden men on active service; it is a remarkable list of men for such a small village.

Private Charles Crowther.

Private Charles Crowther (9906), of the 9th Worcesters, Coronation Cottages, Wilden, near Stourport, died in the Royal Naval Hospital at Malta on February 2nd of wounds received in action at Gallipoli on November 29th, 1915.

Private Crowther was the first man in Wilden to offer his services to his country, and he is the first from this place to fall. In the early part of last year he was sent to France, and after a very short stay was invalided back to England, spending several weeks in hospital at Manchester, where he met with very much kindness from nurses and friends. He sailed for the Dardanelles in September last. He received his wounds (shrapnel in lung and shoulder) while out with a wiring party on November 29th, the day after returning to the trenches, subsequent upon a week in the rest hospital suffering from dysentry.

He was admitted to hospital at Malta on December 8th, dangerously ill with wounds and frostbite, and dysentry in addition. For some time his progress was satisfactory, and great hopes were entertained of his recovery. Nurse Glover (late of Hartlebury) after seeing him on her arrival at Malta in January wrote home:—

PRIVATE C. CROWTHER.

"He is progressing favourably and has been visited by His Excellency the Governor of Malta, who congratulated him on his recovery. He has plenty of fish, chicken, beef tea, etc., and has been told to ask for anything that he would like different. He is able to wash his own hands and face. He had a bottle of lemonade on his locker and told me he had everything he needed."

Mrs. K. Fisher (a lady who also visited him in hospital and very kindly wrote home about him) says in a letter received last Monday:—" I went in to see him last Sunday (January 30th) and took him some tasty eatables and some home-baked scones, which he always enjoyed for tea. He was bright and said he felt fairly well, but I thought he looked pale and weak. I went in to see him again yesterday, and was so grieved to hear he had passed away. He was always so brave and patient, and I liked to talk to him. I feel so sorry for you, for I know how hard it must be for those who are far away from their dear ones. He will be buried to-morrow with all the honours of a soldier's funeral, and if I can possibly secure one I shall send you a photo of the place where he is buried."

At a memorial service held on Sunday at All Saints', Wilden, the Vicar (Rev. W. H. Cory), who took as his text the Fifth Commandment, preached to a crowded congregation composed chiefly of the clerical staff and employees of Messrs. Baldwin's, Limited, and in the course of his sermon mentioned that nothing would better have pleased the founder and benefactor of that church, Mr. Alfred Baldwin—the anniversary of whose death they were that day also commemorating—than to see it being used as it was then being used, to do honour to the memory of a brave man who had given his life for his country.

The deceased, who was forty-four years of age and a native of Wilden, leaves a widow and five children.

Charles' obituary in the Kidderminster weekly newspaper, February 1916.

Opposite The Order of Service for the unveiling of a simple and sombre bronze tablet inside Wilden Church to commemorate the fallen. Stanley Baldwin performed the ceremony on 13 February 1921, the anniversary of his own father's death in 1908, and of Charles' memorial service in 1916.

THE NAMES OF THE
MEN COMMEMORATED ON THE TABLET
ARE:—

CHARLES DUDLEY, Pte. 3rd Worcs. Regt., Missing after the battle of Hooge, Belgium, June 16th, 1915. Aged 22.

CHARLES CROWTHER, Pte. 9th Worcs., Died in Malta, February 2nd, 1916, of wounds received in Gallipoli. Aged 44.

FRANK POWELL, Pte. 7th Worcs., Killed in battle in France, July 19th, 1916. Aged 19.

ERNEST PRITCHARD, Corpl. 10th Worcs., Killed in battle in France, August 1st, 1916. Aged 23.

ARTHUR PRITCHARD, Pte. R.A.M.C., Died at Bournemouth, August 10th, 1916, of wounds received in France. Aged 19.

BERNARD WESLEY PRITCHARD, Pte. 1st Worcs., Accidentally killed nr. Vermelles, France, September 8th, 1916. Aged 19.

HARRY PARRY, 13th Battn. Rifle Brigade, Killed on the Somme, November 14th, 1916. Aged 19.

FREDERICK ROSSER, 13th Battn. Rifle Brigade, Died of wounds in France, November 16th, 1916. Aged 36.

GEORGE HENRY JAMES, 11th Worcs. Regt., Killed in action in Greece, April 24th, 1917. Buried nr. Lake Doiran. Aged 31.

WALLACE MYTTON, Corpl. 116th Canadians, Died June 27th, 1917, at No. 8 Stationary Hospital, France. Aged 23.

JOHN ARTHUR DODD, Pte. 10th Worcs., Killed in battle in France, May 28th, 1918. Aged 21.

Wilden Church.

UNVEILING OF A BRONZE TABLET IN MEMORY OF THE MEN OF WILDEN WHO FELL IN THE GREAT WAR, 1914—1918.

February 13th, 1921.

AT 3 P.M.

MAYWOOD AND SON, TYP BOURNPORT

ORDER OF SERVICE.

— ✠ —

Hymn :

"O God our help in ages past."—A. & M. 165.

— ✠ —

"Greater love hath no man than this that a man lay down his life for his friends."

— ✠ —

Our Father.

O Lord, open Thou our lips, etc.

— ✠ —

PSALM XXIII.

THE Lord is my shepherd: therefore can I lack nothing.

2 He shall feed me in a green pasture; and lead me forth beside the waters of comfort.

3 He shall convert my soul: and bring me forth in the paths of righteousness, for His Name's sake.

4 Yea, though I walk through the valley of the shadow of death, I will fear no evil; for Thou art with me; Thy rod and Thy staff comfort me.

5 Thou shalt prepare a table before me against them that trouble me: Thou hast anointed my head with oil, and my cup shall be full.

6 But Thy loving kindness and mercy shall follow me all the days of my life: and I will dwell in the house of the Lord for ever.

Lesson :

WISDOM III., 1—6.

✠

Magnificat :

Stanford in B♭.

✠

Prayers.

✠

Anthem (H. H. Woodward).

"Sunset and evening star." Lord Tennyson.

A. & M. 694.

— ✠ —

Unveiling of Memorial

BY

THE RIGHT HON.
STANLEY BALDWIN, P.C., M.P.

✠

GOD SAVE THE KING.

❧ PART TWO ❧

Letters

14 July 1915

Pte C Crowther
5th Batt Worcs
Picklecombe Fort
Nr Plymouth

July 14th

Dear Kate, Another line or two [to] let you know that I am quite well. I hope that you and the kiddies are well and all the others. I have not had time to write before we have been so busy. This is a lovely little place right down on the coast under a wood but you can't get out, the gates are locked as soon as anything comes in. and you have to get a pass to go out. There are only five allowed out in one day, but it is alright inside, you can get up on the top of the fort and see for miles out to sea. There are a lot of ships going in and out day and night. Two big Dreadnoughts came in on Sunday morning, one with both her funnels blowed off. The other was damaged as well. We have to do guards here and there are no drills. We have to guard the search lights and our tanks, it is a sight when all the lights are on. From all the forts round here you can see everything as plain as in the day for miles all round. All the ground round here belongs to Lord Edgcombe. There are a lot of peacocks and deer roaming about besides pheasants and rabbits. Try and send me a drink if you can. I have not heard whether you got the parcel or not. It is over a week now, there is only one post a day from here. I go on in the morning till Friday morning then I have done till Sunday. We are not worked hard. We are on two eggs for breakfast in the morning and they have charged 1/9 a dozen for them. What price are they up there. I will try and write again when I come off guards. Tell mother I will send her a line or two as soon as I can. I hope you do not worry but I know that Betty and Arthur take a lot of watching now. Tell Wilfred that I hope he is a good lad and helps to mind them. I hope Harry has got alright,
Goodnight, give them all a kiss for me, yours ever, Charlie.

25 July 1915

Pte Crowther
5th Worcs 9806
Fort Tregantle
Nr Plymouth

[July] Sunday 25

Dear Wife, Just a few lines to let you know that I am quite well, I hope that it will find you all the same, I hope that you keep up yourself. We have been busy here this last week. I went back into the cookhouse as soon as we got back here. It has been raining every day since but it is very hot as well. There are a lot of Kiddy chaps here now. There is one that works at Coombs Wood, he knows Jack [Mayall] well. There is another named Denning, he goes up to Guests, his wife knows you and me but I do not remember her. There has a lot been moved away today, some to Worcester and some to Fareham by Aldershot. Some of the men that are over age for the front have got to go to work in the Army hospitals and some have got to go Malta and Egypt to go on the hospital ships and some have got to help to unload the ships that take the ammunition out. I dont know whether I shall have to move yet or not. They are taking all the names of the men today. I might have to stop on where I am but I should not mind going to Malta for a bit to work. It is a lovely place so they say, them that have been there. We are having a grand living still, all the young potatoes are a fine sample. They are grown close here, we weighed one yesterday and it was a pound and 2 ounces [and] kidney [beans] I hope Harry has got alright again. I shall write to him this week. I want him to get me a form off Mr. Best to show that I was proficient when I left the Volunteers, then I shall get a little bit more pay. I should like to see Betty and Arthur about six at night. I bet they would have a bit of black on their faces. Tell Wilf to write and let me know he is getting on at school, and Marjorie as well. It dont seem 12 months since it started but it will soon be here. I hope mother and dad keep well how are the pigs getting on.
Give them all a kiss and tell them to be good. Good night
Yours ever Charlie
I should have liked to have seen the paper about Mr South

28 July 1915 (to ???)

Pte C Crowther
5th Worcs A co 9806
Fort Tregantle
Nr Plymouth

July 28th
Dear Sister. I am finding a few minutes to answer your last letter and to thank you for sending me what you did. It came in very useful. I hope that you and all the others are quite well, I am myself. There is a lot of moving about lately. I have not been able to let Kate or anyone else know much. We are not to let anyone know the places where we go to. Some have gone away this week. I should have wrote before but I was expecting to be sent away but I didnt know where to. We went to a place for eight days to a fort overlooking Plymouth Breakwater. It was a lovely little spot but a dangerous one for anyone to try to pass to get into Plymouth. There was a Battery of heavy artillery covering every vessel coming in by day and night. And we had to do sentry overlooking the Sound to prevent anyone getting near the wires that fed the search lights. It was a grand sight to see them all on at the same time. You could see the vessels miles out and when they came by they would have to signal before they could enter the Sound. We saw one Dreadnaught convoyed in with both of her funnels blowed off and another with a great hole in the side. We might have to go abroad again but to work at one or the other of the bases. Some are wanted for hospital work and some for unloading ammunition. I dont know whether I shall have to go or not yet for I went back into the cookhouse as soon as we came back. I hope that mother and dad keep well and that Harry has got well again. Could you get me one or two of the pamphlets that the County Council are printing about the Worcesters. I should like one or two if you could. I should like to go to Plymouth on Tuesday if you could help me to but do not send anything if you cant spare it, I dont want you to go short yourself. There are some of the cook's friends coming down from Kidder and Brierley Hill soon that I know and I should like to have a good look round. If I have to go out I think that I shall go to Malta. I should like to see that part very much. Well I hope that we shall have better news this Bank Holiday than we did last for there [are] a lot of fine fellows here that will be crippled for life but still they talk of going out again. In fact some have volunteered but the doctor will not pass them. I have seen several that went out [to France] when I did and they are all wounded, some badly. I suppose that Mollie is alright or else Kate would have let me know. Well, goodnight and remember me to all from your loving brother Charles
Excuse this scribble.

[Mollie was Harry's little daughter, slightly younger than Marjorie]

27 August 1915

9806 A Company 5th Worcs
Tregantle
Plymouth

Dear Wife, I received your letter last night. I had just gone up to post [to you] when the postman gave it to me. I was very pleased to hear that you are keeping well. I have been up for an inspection this afternoon. I am marked fit but I don't know yet where I have got to go to. It might be France, Egypt or anywhere else for all I know yet. I like the name very well, it will suit her very well. Send me a shilling or two by return, I want to send a little parcel home. I have not picked much up this month. I have been talking it over this afternoon with the Pay Master and he says that he will write to Warwick this next Monday and see about it. I will write again on Monday and let you know if I have got the money. I can get to know myself. How is Dick Bradley going on, Give my love to them all and kiss them for me. Good night, yours ever, Charlie.
Excuse scribble, in a hurry.

15 September 1915

[Around Sept 15]
Dear Wife, just a line or two to let you know that I am quite well. I hope that all of you are the same. I got your letter alright and one from Sue this morning. I can't tell you when I am going away yet, we had to go before the doctor again this morning to see if we were all fit but we were not told when we should have to go. I am sending a few things back. The overalls will come in for me when I get back which I think I shall alright. I hope that you and the kiddies will keep going on the right way now. I hope that dear little Arthur's cough is better altogether by now. I was sorry to [hear] about Alice. I hope that she has got better. I will send as soon as I can when I know the day of going to the Dardanelles. We have our orders to Stand By but we are not fitted out. That takes about three days to kit the lot of us so it wont be this week. I will write a line or two to mother in the morning if I can get a few minutes quiet but there is not much chance. Give Wilf the brush, we have to [comb ur] hair. I will send my shoes the last thing when I know for good. Good night and give them all a big kiss,
Yours ever Charlie

20 September 1915

Sept 20th 1915

Dear Wife, just another line or two to let you know that I am still here. We have been Standing To since last Wednesday it is tiring I can tell you. We have to have our rifles and packs and baggage by us from morning to night so it is not very pleasant waiting like this. The soldiers regret they have not given it us yet. I hope that you keep going on alright and the other little ones. I have just scribbled these few lines to let you know that I am here. I will try and send again tomorrow. I want to send another parcel with my shoes in but I dont want to go out [abroad] without any money in my pocket. If you will send 1/6 I will get them sent on. I have not been able to go outside nor are the others that are going out quite soon. Tell Wilf get it and send on by the first post then I will send it right away. Must close or shall miss post goodnight and God bless you all. Your loving husband Charlie

21 September 1915 (before sailing)

Devonport postmark, 7.45 pm
Stourport post mark

(September 21st)

Dear Wife, received your letter last night. Was glad to know you were all going on the right way. We have not got our final orders yet but we expect to go on Saturday morning. We have got all our new clothes and helmets and been inspected by the General so we shant be long any way now. I will send you my fresh address as soon as we have got it. It will take us three weeks sail to get there. We shall have a nice little voyage and I hope that we shall get safe back. Glad you have had the little one christened and that Arthur stood to it. I will on as soon as we get our orders. This is all the time, so send another remember me to them all and keep a good heart till I get home again,
Your loving husband Charlie.

[Arthur Bourne, Dora Kate's young nephew, stood as godfather]

22 September 1915

Sept 22nd

Dear Wife, I have just received your letter. It is just in time for we start today at half past one for Devonport to be on the ship for three. I hope that you wont worry for I dont think that some of us will go any further than the base. It has been rough out there lately but there will be a turn someday, for it cant go on at this rate for a great while longer for they must be losing a lot more than we are. I hope that you will keep well now, and the kiddies till I get back. I will write as soon as I can after we have

1 View from the vicarage grounds, looking across the school and church to Wyre Mill Farm, with the outskirts of Stourport beyond. (Courtesy of Ray Carpenter)

2 The Stour, painted from the Sling, which is the footpath running along the river from Wyre Mill Farm to the railway bridge just below the old Rock Tavern. (Courtesy of Ray Carpenter)

3 East Window, (Altar).
St Martin, Our Lord, Saint George, 1902: the gift of Alfred and Louisa Baldwin.

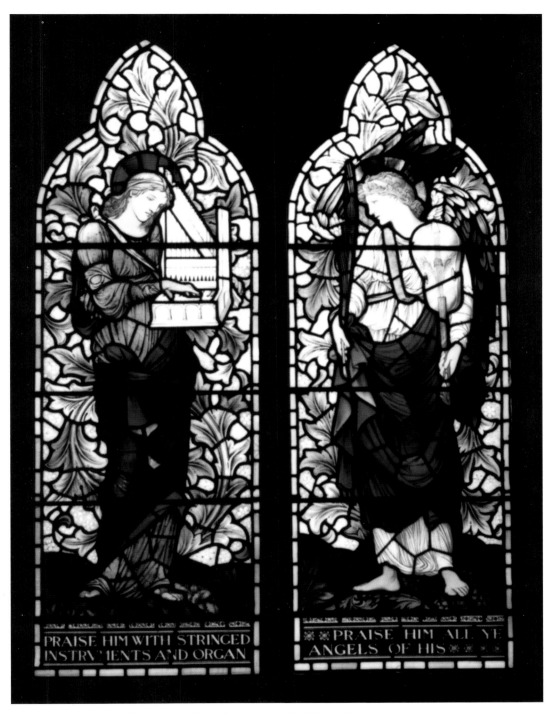

4 Saint Cecilia and the Minstrel Angel, 1902: the gift of Roger Beck.

5 Foliage and Joshua, 1909:
given by the Directors of
Baldwins Ltd., in memory of
their Chairman. The foliage is
also dedicated to the memory
of Louisa Baldwin.

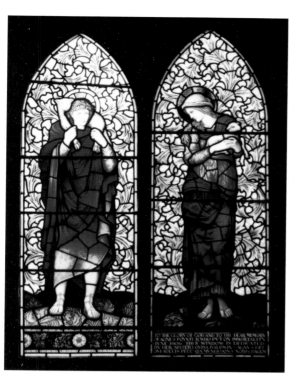

6 Miriam, 1902: the gift of Roger Beck.
Saint Agnes, 1907: in memory of Lady Agnes
Pointer.

7 Samuel and Timothy, 1909: in memory of
William Gordon Felton.

8 Fortitude and Triumph (King Ethelbert), 1903: in memory of Edward Arthur Baldwin.

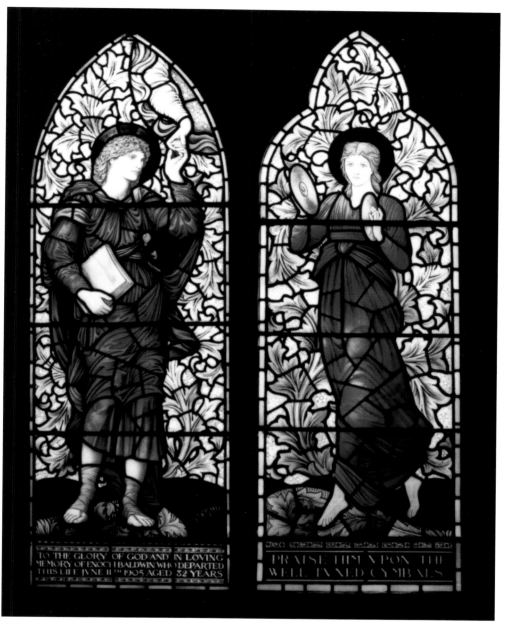

9 The Good Shepherd, 1914.
   Enoch, 1907: in memory of Enoch Baldwin.

10   West Window. A Paradise of Angels, 1904: in memory of Bishop Philpott, Dean Butler, John Haviland, Rector of Hartlebury, Henry Nash and Elisha Smith, both of Liverpool, and John Saunders of Cookley.

started. We shall sail to Malta so you will get one as soon as I can send it. Remember me to all at home, and Alice and Harry. Tell Shammy that I hope to have a drink at Tippers at Christmas if I have a bit of luck.

Well I must close now, we have got to parade in a few minutes. Tell Wilf to be a good lad and send me a card to let me know how he is getting on at school. I should like to have a photo of the lot of you if you can [get] one. Goodbye for the present

Your loving husband

Charlie

Keep your pecker up

28 September 1915

RECEIVED FROM HM FORCES
NO CHARGE TO BE MADE

28/9/15

Dear Wife, just a line or two to let you know that I am going on alright at present. We are somewhere on the briny not far from Gib. Hoping you and the kiddies are well, also those at home. I am still your loving husband Charlie.

1 October 1915

CENSORED

1st October HMS Majestic

Dear Wife, A few lines to let you know that I am still quite well I hope that you and the children are the same. We have had a fair journey so far, it has been interesting to me as well. I wish we had been going on a more pleasant job then we could have had lighter thoughts. I hope that when we get there that we shall be able to do our bit and come out on top. Well Kate if I get hit I hope it wont be so bad that I cant come and see you all again. I hope that it will soon be ended for the sake of the country as well as ourselves. Remember me to mother and dad and all the others. Tell Wilf that I want him to be a good lad and look after the others till I get back again which I hope to do before long. Time has fled it dont seem long since I was there but it is over 2 months since I left everyone the last time. Give them all a good kiss for me. Good night and God bless you all, Yours ever Charlie

Pte C Crowther 9806 9th Worcs
British Mediterranean Force Dardanelles

Just had a look at Arthur and the other two

7 October 1915

CENSORED

7/10/15

Dear Wife, A few lines to let you know that I am quite well, I hope that you and the children are the same. We have got to the end of our journey on this ship, we are now in the harbour. I do not know how long we have got to stop here, I dont think it will be long before we move off. We have had a good voyage it has been interesting. Tell Wilf I will write a letter to him as soon as I have the chance. Give my love to them all. Tell the kiddies to be good till I come back. It is a bit hot here now. I should like to see the little one I hope she will grow the right way. I must close now so good bye for present and keep your pecker up, your loving husband Charlie

Pte C Crowther 9806 9th Batt Worcs Regt
13th Division Mediterranean Force, Dardanelles

Tell mother I will write her as soon as I can.
I hope that Wilf helps you a bit.

12 October 1915

9806 Pte C Crowther
Of the 9th Batt Worcs
13th Div 39th Brigade
British Med Exped Force

12/10/15

Dear Wife I got off the boat last night and we went straight up to the trenches, they were firing all the time, it was a bit rough getting there but we got there alright. I am writing these few lines while the shells are going over us. I hope that you and the kiddies keep well. I am quite well myself at present, I will write again as soon as I have a chance. We are having it warm days but it is cold nights. Give them all a kiss for me,
        Goodbye for the present Charlie

12 October 1915

[12 Oct]

Dear Wife, just a few lines to let you know that I am fit and well. I hope that you and the kids are well, also mother and dad and all the others. Well we have got here at last. We were on the boat 19 days, we got off the boat last night and marched straight to the trenches. They were firing all the time. The big guns made a tidy noise and the rifle fire was terrific. We had a pleasant journey out here, it was a bit crowded but still it was a good trip. We stayed in the harbour here three days and a sight it was to see all the vessels that were here, some of all sorts. Well I hope that you wont worry, but cheer up and get that little one [into] a big one against I get back. I suppose Arthur is getting a big boy now. I have a look at him every day and Wilf and Marj. I suppose that Betty has got a big girl now and takes a bit of minding. How are Fred Rosser and the others getting on. I have not seen a paper for a long time now except in Devon. Did you get my other shoes and jersey.

There are a lot of Kidder chaps up here. I hope that we have a bit of luck and get safe through with it. There are a few flies in these trenches, you cant work for them. How are dad's pigs, I trust they are nice ones by now. I must close now. They are dropping a few shells over now but we cant see what damage they are doing. Well, goodbye for the present from your loving husband Charlie.

Private C Crowther
9806 Aco 9th Battalion Worcs Reg
British Med Exped Force

Good luck to all of you.

15 October 1915

Oct 15th

Dear Wife, Another line or two to let you know that I am going on alright up till the present. I hope that you and all the others are the same. We are still in the trenches with the shells flying over but they have not done much damage to us at this spot, the flies are more terrible to us than the Turks for there are millions of them and the Turks keep in hiding and snipe at us so it dont give us much chance to fire back at them, in fact they dont show themselves at all. I saw young Cox from Toston and he told me that Bert Cope had gone into hospital. I dont know what is the matter with him but he is not wounded. I daresay we shall be here for a tidy bit, but there is no knowing when we shall make an advance. Tell Alice that I will write her a line or two as soon as I can get a chance but writing in the trench is not like writing at Barracks. You have only got room to turn around and duck when the bullets and shells come over. The Turks are sending one or two over now but they are not very big ones. I should like a paper for I have not seen one since we left Tregantle so you see we dont know how the war is going on in France or here for that matter.

I hope that mother and dad keep well and will keep so till I can see them again. It is very hot here days, but very cold nights. It is what they call their winter now. It is all hills round here covered with trenches, but our Navy shells it every day and night and they can tell the distance to a few yards and they are from three to five miles away.

I hope Wilf is a good boy and helps you and gets on well at school. You havent told me how he is going on with it. I should like him and his Aunty Alice to see this country,

it would interest them both. We have our water from one of the wells what you read of in Scripture. Has Marj got her figs now. I should like to see her eat one again. How does Arthur like going to school, has he started to learn anything yet. I suppose Betty has to mind the baby a lot. Give them all a good kiss for me and tell them to be good children till I get home again. Give my love to all the others and keep well till I see you all again.
Your loving husband Charlie.

Pte C. Crowther
9806 9th Batt Worcs Regt
13th Division 39th Brigade
British Med Exped Force

22 October 1915 (to ???)

22 Oct
Dear Sister, a few lines to let you know that I am quite well. We are still in the trenches in front of the enemy. We are not far from them, but we cant see them, they are under cover the same as us. I cant tell you anything about this place. We are not allowed to mention names. Give my love to Mother and Father and to Harry and Lizzie. It is very cold nights here now. I hope that we shall get it over now and get back safe again,
        Your loving brother Charles

26 October 1915

Oct 26th
Dear Wife just a line or two to let you know that I am still quite well, I hope it will find you and the kids the same. I hope that the little ones have got over the whooping cough. I should like to see them all again but it dont look like it just yet. We have heard there will be a move pretty soon. It is very cold nights here especially in the firing line you have got to [be] up and at it all the time. We came up into the firing trenches again yesterday for another turn for a day or two then we go back into the reserve ones for a rest. There have been plenty of shells flying about but they have missed us so far. Tell mother that you will have to send my plum pudding and cake out here between you. Send them out in the tins then they wont get broke. Pack them in a wooden box and fill it in tight. Sue will help you to do it. It would not be any good of sending any meat or anything like that for it would get spoiled before it got here it is such a distance to here. We are not allowed to mention the names of places so I cant tell you where we are but we have not gone much farther than when we got here first. I should like to have the paper sent every week for you cant get any news here, There is not a building in

sight for miles only a few ruined huts what have been blown down by the shells. Well, I hope that you and all the others will keep well and myself and get back safe to be with you once again. It seems a long time since I was there, it will be a treat to have a comfortable sleep once again. I hope that Wilf keeps a good lad and helps you to a few things. Does Marj help to do anything or does she do a jig or two. I suppose that Arthur has to have him a bit of play as usual. I should like to see him. I have a look at him pretty often. Tell Betty that her dad will soon be back again to take her out. Well I must close now give my love to them all and kiss the kids for me and tell them to be good.
Goodbye for the present and good luck to us all,
from your loving husband, Charlie

Pte C Crowther 9806 9th Batt Worcs Rgt
13th Div 39th Brigade British Mediterranean Exped. Force

They are dropping a few over now [scribbled on the bottom]

29 October 1915

29th Oct
Dear Wife, Just a few lines to let you know that I am still quite well. I hope this will find you and all the others the same. It is pretty quiet here except for shellfire and that comes very thick all the time.
I hope that you have got alright again and got your strength again. If you send a parcel out you might put me a bit of good cheese in and a new pipe. We get plenty of tobacco but we have not had any cheese since we left the boat. It is a job to get anything up here for they are under fire all the time they are bringing the food up from the beach. They have to bring it all up in the night time and then they are being fired at all the time. How are Syd and Sarah, and Jack Tipper getting on. I should like to have an hour or two on the green with them. I have not had a paper or letter since we left for here, but it takes three weeks to come so I dont expect one yet. You must send out at once for me to get it by Christmas for fear I should get moved but it dont look like it yet.
Living in the trenches is not like being at home, you have not to get and make yourself a cup of tea, Its a job to get enough water to drink. We have managed to get a good wash and shave this morning and feel a lot better for it.
I hope that dad has not done himself up by working in the garden and looking after them pigs. I hope that he has had a good crop of potatoes and other stuff, for it will be dear for a long time yet. How are they going on at the forge. I expect they have plenty to do now on Government orders. Tell Shammy I shall be able to drink a [whole] brewing myself if we can get back safe, for we have not seen any since we left Tregantle.
Well, I must close now for they are collecting them up now. Give my love to them all and give the kiddies a good kiss for me and keep a bit cheerful till I get back again. Is the

little one alright, I hope it will be growing well. I should like to see it now. Goodbye for the present, your loving husband Charlie.

Pte C. Crowther
9806 9th Batt Worcs Regt
39th Brigade 13th Division
British Med Exped Force

2 November 1915

November 2nd
Dear Kate, Just a few lines to let you know that I am still quite well. We are still up in the firing lines but there is not much going on yet. We are somewhere in Gallipoli but I cannot say where. I hope that you and all the others are well. I suppose that you are having it a bit colder now. It is hot here days, but cold at night. How is Arthur Bourne going on with his lot. There are a lot of Territorials come out here and they will be wanted before we can make much of a move for there is a lot of ground to be taken. We have to go out at night and dig trenches to get nearer to them. We had a Church service on Sunday morning in our line of trenches. The bullets and shells were flying over our heads all the time but no one was hit. It looks as if it is going to be a longer job than we thought. At first I thought that we might be at home for Christmas but it dont look like it now. Tell Alice and Mother that I will try and send them a line when I have got another chance. I must close this now for some of us have got to go out now. Tell the kiddies to be good and not worry you till I get back. Remember me to Mother and Dad and all the others, and good luck to us all,
I remain your loving husband Charlie.
Excuse scribble

Pte C. Crowther
9806 9th Batt Worcs Reg
13 Division 39 Brigade
Brit Med Exped Force

Dont forget to give the little one a bit of a cuddle from me.
I should like to see them all again soon.

5 November 1915

5/11/15
Pte C. Crowther 9806 9th Batt Worcs Regt
13th Div 39th Brigade British Med Exped Force

Dear Kate, another line or two to let you and the others at home know that I am still quite well. I hope that the kiddies have got alright again. I know you have had a handful with them but I hope it is better.

I have not had any news since we left Tregantle but it takes three weeks at the least to get here so I cannot expect any for another week yet if you get mine in the same time. I cannot write a lot for we have not got to mention any thing about our movements out here. We have not had much rifle fire, but plenty of shells both day and night. We cant see them for they are in trenches the same as us. We have been making some more trenches to get nearer to them so I expect we shall be having a go at them soon. If you send anything out pack it up tight for there are some that come up here with all the stuff took out. There was one came yesterday that was sent out in August but that one was alright. I hope that Wilf is a good lad and helps you as much as he can. I suppose that Betty minds the baby for you in her way. I hope that mother and dad keep well. I cannot write to you all for there is not time for writing for we have got to be on the lookout all the time day and night. Give my love to them all and kiss the kids for me, your loving husband Charlie.

9 November 1915

Nov 9th

Dear Wife, Another few lines to let you know that I am still quite well, I hope that you and the family are all the same. We are still at the same place, it is hot days but cold nights, it is a lot different sleeping in the trenches to what it is in bed but I hope to be there and have a good sleep before much longer if all goes well. I suppose that the kiddies are thinking about Christmas now. I hope that they will have a merry one and all of us have a new year better than this one. Well I cant write a lot for we have not got to put anything in about the places out here. I hope that you got the last parcel from Tregantle alright, I have not had a letter or paper yet not up to the time of writing this, but its hardly time yet it takes a long time to reach us here. Tell Alice I have not been able to write to her yet but I will send her a line or two as soon as I can. How does Arthur get on at school. Is he a good lad to get there early, but I suppose that is a bit of a job to get them ready. How does Betty get on with them, is she boss. How does the little one come on. I should like to see them all together again.

Well I must close now, we are going out trench digging again. Give my love to them all, and a merry Christmas to us all. Kiss them all for me and tell them that I hope to be back once again. Goodbye for the present, your loving husband Charlie.

Pte C Crowther
9806 Aco 9th Batt Worcs Regt
39th Brigade 13th Division
Brit Med Exped Force

15 November 1915

Nov 15th

Dear Kate just a few lines to let you know that I am still quite well, I hope this will find you and the kids the same. I hope that mother and dad are well also. I hope that you dont worry yourself a lot but I know that you have got your hands full now. I hope you will be able to get on alright now. It seems a long while since I saw you all, but we must hope for the best and pray that it will soon be over, and that we may all get safe home soon. We are having a lot of stuff [fire] out here, we have been at it all the time since we came out. We are trench digging and in the firing line day and night. I have been out the last two nights with the evening party, it is a bit dangerous, but it all is out here, for the shells are dropping all day long. You have to keep under cover as much as you can for you dont know what way they will burst. Our navy have given them a good shelling this last day or two up on the hills, but they will want some taken out. It will have to be done.

How is Shammy getting on, does he get his bit of comfort now or does he mind the fort. I have only seen one old paper since we came out, that was a month old. I should like to have a brewing again. I have not had a letter yet but hope to get one by the next mail. You might get Wilf to write a letter or postcard twice a week then I shall be sure of getting one. They get them twice a week but they take three weeks to come, so if I missed the one mail I should get it in the other. Well I must close now for it is time for them [letters] to be in. Tell the kids that I am thinking of them and you all the time. I hope that you will have a merry Christmas for it will soon be here now. I should like a new pipe if you can send me one. We get plenty of tobacco but we have not had any beer since we started so you can tell I could do with one. Remember me to them all and give the kids a kiss and the baby a cuddle from me, and good luck to us all,

Your loving husband Charlie.

Pte C. Crowther

9806 Aco 9th Batt Worcs Regt

13th Division 39th Brigade

Early November 1915 (from Kate)

Early November, Wilden

Dear Charlie I am writing these few lines hoping they will find you alright as we are at home. Their coughs are better and Arthur has gone to school, I am very glad for he is an artful little hound and very mischiefful, so is Betty. I have shortened [taken out of long gowns] the baby she is a nice little kid, she is so like Arthur and has got a head of hair for a baby just the same as Arthur. The kids want to see you again. They do seem to be having it rough everywhere, it seems a long time coming to a close. The price of everything is awful since this last budget. I got your postcard. I thought it was no use writing so soon, it does seem a long time getting to hear from you but I suppose we must wait a

bit for your usual letter. Let me know if I can send you a little bit of something. Coal has rose again. It is a job to manage now I can tell you. Your dad's pigs are doing well. I wish I had one to come in this winter if you could share it, I hope you will next time. Your mother and dad are very well, they have just had their place done through so they are quite smart. I have just been to see them, the first time in six months, I have got no chance to stir it is a handful I can tell you. I shall be glad when you come home to help me with them. They all wish to be remembered to you. The kids send a kiss. Hope to see you soon,
Yours ever Kate.
Write as soon as possible and let me know.

Mid-November 1915 (from Kate)

[About 20 November, Wilden]
Dear Charlie, Just a few lines in answer to your letter. Was glad to know you were safe and well and hope and trust you will keep so. The children are keeping very well except in colds. You did not say you had heard from me. I have wrote, and so has Mrs. Baldwin, to tell you she has sent a pudding. I will send you a cake; we are sending a parcel between us. Today Dick Bradley has been from France for six days. He looks none the worse for it. I hope you look as well. The baby is coming on well. She is a little beauty; she is a sweet little kid to look at. She is not vaccinated; I wish she was done and well. Arthur is a little tinker. Alice is taking him to Kidder on Saturday for his birthday. I cant keep him in trousers and boots. I have just had Wilf's boots soled and heeled, they are 3/3 it is awful the price of everything now, everything is double so you can tell I have got enough with five of them. I have not got your shoes, they have not sent them. Who could I write to about them that are trusting to a pal. They were your best. Arthur [Bourne] is on Salisbury Plain finishing their training I suppose. Louie wants a lot of minding, as does Betty. Betty is a nice little girl. They [Wilf and Marj] are getting on well at school. Your mother and dad keep very well indeed. I hope you will soon be back with us and all settled down again. The kids all send a big kiss. They seem to want to see you more than ever,
        Yours Kate
I hope you will have good luck

Early December 1915 (from Kate)

The first week of December 1915
Dear Charlie I received your last two letters together, was glad to hear you were alright as we are at home. Baby [Louisa] has had bronchitis but is well again. I am going to have her vaccinated she is 17 weeks old now. It will be a handful, I shall be very glad for you to be at home again to help me with them you dont get much help off relations. Arthur

[Bourne] is going to France on the 3rd of December, they are very near mad about it, but what is theirs to mine? I dont say much about it. I think the more.

Old Joe Randle is marrying his housekeeper on Saturday, quite a small affair. Mrs Jay in the public [pub] is very ill indeed. What about the closing of the public houses. I was thinking what a lot I should have of you at home. Now the work is very bad at Wilden at present, they are only doing 2 or 3 turns a week. And things are awful dear and keep getting worse. I have got enough to do to keep them tidy I can tell you. They are wondering if you will hang your stocking up at Christmas. I did not get your last parcel with your shoes in it; I have been worried about it never coming. Never mind, I would sooner you come instead; you could soon get some more. I would write about them if I knew who to write to. The kids are all growing well. The little one is a picture. You will be delighted with her she is sharp as a needle. Arthur and Betty talk a lot about their Dad. You had better write to Mrs. Baldwin and thank her for your pudding. If you get a chance send a postcard to Mollie. The kids are anxious to have something from out there when you have a chance. How do you get on for money now? Mine dont last long. I must close now with love from all, yours Kate. The kids send a kiss for you.

8 December 1915

Dec 8

Dear Wife just a few lines to let you know how I am getting on. I have been ill since I wrote to you last I was in the rest hospital for a week with dysentery then the very next day I was struck by a piece of shrapnel on the right shoulder and it went down into my stomach. It was a bit rough for the first day or two for we could not lie down at all. I was hit on the Monday morning the 29th and they managed to get us down onto the boat on Saturday 4th. We have got to Malta now so I shall have it seen to now, it is not very much.

The weather was awful out there the last fortnight it rained in in torrents flooded us out of the trenches on the Friday 26th, then it followed up with a blizzard next day with frost at night nearly all of us have got frostbite as well. I hope that you and the kiddies are well and the others as well. You will be able to send here for Christmas. It is not quite so far as the other place. If you have sent out there I shall not get that but some of the other poor devils will. I must close now, your loving husband Charlie. Dont forget to kiss them all a time or two for me. I hope to see them before much longer.

Royal Naval Hospital
East 2 Ward
Bighi
Malta

15 December 1915

Private C. Crowther 9806
9th Worcesters
Royal Naval Hospital
East 2 Ward
Bighi, Malta

Thursday Dec 15th
Dear Wife,

Just a few lines to let you know I am going on satisfactory. I am still weak and they have not extracted the bullet yet. I hope you and the children are all quite well and also mother and father and brothers and sisters. Dear Wife, we are all well looked after here and I am a lot stronger than what I was. I have not received the letters yet, I suppose they are following me about. I hear there is some talk about sending us to England in which [case] I hope so. Dear wife I wish you and the children and all the family a Merry Xmas and a Happy New Year, and I sincerely hope to be with you before very long. Well I have no more news this time so I will close with best love to all from
XXX   Your Loving Husband   XXX
XXX   Charlie   XXX

26 December 1915 (from hospital staff)

Royal Naval Hospital
Bighi, Malta
Dec 26th 1915

Dear Mrs. Crowther

I suppose you will have heard from your husband telling you of his arrival in the above hospital. He is suffering from shrapnel wound of the chest and these last few days he has been far from well so I wanted to write so that you know of his condition. It may yet be necessary for him to undergo an operation, but if such is the case I shall write at once to let you know. I will keep you informed of his condition. Everything is being done for him that can be done and I hope he will pull through, but the doctor is anxious about him at present. I saw him this afternoon and he said he felt easier and had not so much pain.

I will write to you again in a day or two and let you know how he is. I know what an anxiety it is for those who are far from their loved ones.

I remain
Sincerely yours
Mrs. Kathleen Fisher

12 January 1916 (from Kate)

To Private Crowther
  9th Worcesters
  East 2 Ward
  Royal Naval Hospital 12th Jan
  Bighi, Malta

Dear Charlie, in answer to yours which I was very glad to get, to know how you are, since it was three weeks since I heard. I hope and trust you will soon be able to get to England once more. I expect it has been a worry to you to receive nothing from me, but I have sent every week since you left England, so has Wilfred sent some, and Bill Bourne [Shammy] sent you. I had a small parcel come on Christmas Eve addressed to me but when I opened it it was tobacco and matches and a nice new pipe so I thought it looked like yours instead. Bill Tipper's wife had sent it for you, so had I better send it out or not. We had a very quiet Christmas so I tell the children we will have ours when you can come home. They do all look well you will be pleased with them. Louie has just been vaccinated a week today, she has been very cross. She is five months in a fortnight and is going on alright. Arthur was still in the 14th Welsh when he went out, I think I told you he was quarter master. Your mother and dad keep very well considering their age. Betty does talk a lot about her dad and the chocolate she is going to have when you come home, Arthur is going to Stourport with you to buy nuts because they got none at Christmas. I have not been to Kidderminster since you went back after you were over. I will send you some papers if you are well enough to read them. Be sure and look after yourself and make haste and come home once more and help mind the kids again. They all send their love and some kisses but want to see you again. I think this is all this time, yours ever Kate.

Marjorie has a few figs left, so have Betty and Arthur.

15 January 1916 (from Mr Cory)

Wilden Parsonage
Stourport

Jan 15th 1916

Dear Mr. Crowther,
        We have been very sorry to hear how ill you have been and I hope you will continue to improve. Your wife has been very anxious but she has been plucky and hopeful, and I think Wilfred has been a good boy. I enclose a bit from the Wilden Almanac of Wilden men on service, it does not include those waiting to be called up in

their groups. Mrs. Cory sends her kind remembrances in the hope that you will soon be able to travel and get back to home.

May God bless and help you,

Believe me,

Yours faithfully

W.H. Cory

9 January 1916 (British Red Cross)

BRITISH RED CROSS
AND
ORDER OF ST JOHN

ENQUIRIES DEPARTMENT
FOR
WOUNDED AND MISSING

19th January 1916

8 CARLTON HOUSE TERRACE

Dear Madam,

Red Cross Malta has called asking us to inform you C Crowther 5th att 9th Worcesters - condition still serious but his progress is satisfactory - Hoping to be able to send you a better report in a few days,

Yours faithfully,

Louis Mallet,

PP......

31 January 1916

3/1/16

Dear Wife
Just a few lines to let you know that I am getting a bit stronger. I have not been [for] the operation yet but they have had the x/rays on me taken. I dont think they can trace

the bullet yet. It has healed up in my shoulder where it went in, I cant feel anything at all from that. I dont think you had better send anything else out there it might get lost like the other stuff that has been sent out. There were two transports sunk with parcels and letters before I got hit so I suppose mine was amongst the lot. I have had a letter from Mr. Cory. Tell dad to remember me to him. I hope that you and all the kids keep well. I should like to see them again. This letter must do for you all this time for I cannot write very well yet, it makes my fingers ache doing this bit. That was the first letter I had since the day we sailed, it was very welcome. Let me know what Brigade Arthur's lot have joined. Tell mother and dad I can't write this week but I hope you will send me plenty of news now. Remember me to Alice and all the lot of them. Goodnight and God bless you all till I get over there again. Give all the kids a good kiss and tell them to be good,

       Your loving husband
         Charlie

Pte C Crowther 9806
9th Worcs,
Royal Naval Hosp etc.

[Charles wrote 3/1/16 but the letter is definitely 31/1/16)

2 February 1916 (from hospital staff)

                        R N Hospital, Bighi
                              Malta

Feb 2nd
Dear Mrs. Crowther,

      By the time this letter reaches you, you will know of the death of your husband, but I feel I must write you a line or two as my whole sympathy goes out to you. When I wrote to you before he seemed to have much improved, but a great deal of matter accumulated at the lung and an operation was necessary, this being the only chance of saving his life. The operation, we knew, would be a serious one, and he passed quickly away shortly after. I went in to visit him on Sunday and took him some tasty eatables and some home-baked scones which he always enjoyed for tea. He seemed bright and said he felt fairly well, but I thought he looked pale and weak. I went in to see him yesterday again* and was so grieved to hear he had passed away. He was always so brave and patient and I always liked to talk to him. I feel so sorry for you for I know how hard it must be for who are far away from their dear ones. He will be buried tomorrow with all the honours of a soldier's funeral and if I possibly can secure one, I shall send you a photo of the place where he is buried

      With my deepest sympathy,

I remain,

Yours very sincerely

(Mrs) Katherine Fisher

[She must have written this letter around midnight on 2 February, which would account for date discrepancy. Charles died on 2 February and was buried on the 3rd]

4 February 1916 (from the Naval Chaplain)

R.N. Hospital
Bighi, Malta

Feb 4th 16

Dear Mrs. Crowther,

You will have heard by now from the Admiralty authorities of the death of your husband Charles Crowther (Pte 5th Worcesters) in this hospital. He died on Feb 2nd from wounds in action and operation shock. It was my sad duty to bury him Feb 3rd at 4 pm in the Royal Naval Cemetery Bighi. I thought you would like to know that this cemetery is situated in a beautiful part of the Island and is very well kept by the Navy, I send you my very sincere sympathy in your sad bereavement.

Believe me,

Yours sincerely,

H. G. Heap

Chaplain R.N.

[Charlie's change of battalion had not been passed on to the chaplain]

1st Oct Dear Wife A few lines to let you know that I am still quite well I hope that you and the kiddies are the same. We have had a fair journey so far it has been interesting to me as well. I wish we had been going on a more pleasanter Job than we could have had lighter thoughts. I hope that when we got there that we shall be able to do our bit and come out on top. Well that if I get hit I hope it wont be so bad that I cant come and see you all again. I hope that it will soon be ended for the sake of the country as well as our selves. Remember me to mother and dad, and all the others. Tell Wilf that I want him to be a good lad and look after the others till I get back again which I hope to do before long, time has fled it dont seem long since I was there but it is over nine months since I left you the last time give them all a good kiss for me. Goodnight and god bless you all your ever Charlie

Pte C. Crowther 9806 9th Worcesters
British Mediteranean Force
Dardenelles

Just had a look at Arthur, and the other two.

Dear Wife just a few lines to
let you know that I am fit
and well I hope that you and
the kiddies are well, also mother
and dad and all the others.
Well we have got here at last.
we were on the boat 19 days
we got off last night and
marched straight to the
trenches they were firing
all the time the big guns
made a tidy noise and the
rifle fire was terrific. We had
a pleasant journey out here, it
was a bit crowded but still
it was a good trip. We stayed
in the harbour here three days

and a sight it was to see all
vessels that were here some of all
sorts. Well I hope that you wont
worry but cheer up and get
that little one a big one against
I get back for I long to see her.
I suppose Arthur is getting a big
boy now. I have a look at him
every day. and Milly and Marge.
I suppose that Betty has got a
big girl by now and takes a
bit of minding. How are Fred
Rosser and the others going on
I have not seen a paper for a
long time now except Berrow.
did you get my other shoes
and guersey.

There are a lot of Riddon
chaps up here I hope that
we have a bit of luck and
get safe through with it. There
are a few flies in these trenches
you cant wait for them How
are dads pigs going on I should
they are nice ones by now.
I must close now they are
coming round for them now.
they are dropping a few shells
over now ~~they~~ but
we cant see what damage
they are doing. Well good bye
for the present, from your loving
husband Charlie

November 2nd

Dear Kate, A few lines to let you know
that I am still quite well. We are still
up in the firing line but there is not much
going on yet. We are somewhere in Gallipoli
but I can't say where. I hope that you and
all the others are well. I suppose that
you are having it a bit colder now.
It is hot here days but cold at night.
How is Arthur Bourne going on with his lot
There are a lot of Territorials come out here and
they will be wanted before we can make
much of a move for there is a lot of
ground to be taken. We have to go out
at night and dig trenches to get in
them. We had a Church Service
morning in our line of trenches th—
and shells were flying over our he—
time but no one hit. It looks as if—
going to be a longer job than—
at first I thought that we might—
home for Christmas but it don't—
like it now. Tell Alice and B—
that I will try and send them—
or two when I have got another—

I must close this now for some of
us have got to go out now. Tell the
kiddies to be good and not to worry
you till I get back. Remember me to
Mother and Dad and all the others
and good luck to us all I remain
your loving husband Charlie
excuse scribble

Pte C Crowther
9306 A co 9th Batt Worcs Regt
13 Division 39th Brigade
British Med Exped Force

Dont forget to give the little one
a bit of a cuddle for me. I should
like to see them all again soon

... it takes a long time to
... ackues here. Tell Alice I
... ve not been able to write
her yet but I will sent
... a line or two as soon as
... can. How does Arthur get
... at school is he a good
... d to get there early too
... ppose that it is a bit of a
... bita get them ready however
... Betty get on with them
... he Bon. How does the little
... cave on. I should like to
... them all together again

Nov 9th

Dear Wife Another few lines to
let you know that I am
still quite well. I hope that
you and all the family
are the same. We are still at
the same place it is hot day
but cold at night it is a
lot different sleeping in the
trenches to what it is in
but I hope to be there and
a good sleep before much
longer if all goes well. I say

Nov 15th

Dear Kate Just a few lines to let
you know that I am still quite
well. I hope that this will find
you and the children the same.
I hope that mother and dad
are well also. I hope that you
don't worry yourself a lot
but I know that you have
got your hands full now
but I hope that you will be
able to get on allright from
now. It seems a long while
since I saw you all last but
we must hope for the best
and pray that it will soon be
over and that we may all get
safe home again soon.

We are having it a bit stiff out
here. we have been at it all the
time since we came out. We are
trench digging, and in the firing
line day and night. I have
been out the last two nights
with the wiring party, it is a bit
dangerous. but it all is out here
for the shell are dropping all day
long you have to keep under
cover as well as you can. for
you don't know which way they
will burst. Our navy have given
them a good shelling this last
day or two up on the hills, but
they will want some taken
but it will have to be done.

... flaming, Salmon with
... get his bit of comfort
... he mind the fowl. I
... seen one old paper
... came out that was a
... I should like to have
... ain I have not had a
... hope to get one
... mail you might
... into a letter or a
... a week then I sha...
... this one. they get
... week out here
... three week to
... minded the
... at bit the other.
... more far it is
... Tell the hub...
... hers of them
... I hope that

---

that the kiddies are think...
about christmas now I...
that there will have a...
one and all of us hav...
happier new year better than
this one I hope. Well I cant
write a lot for we have not
got to just anything in about
the places, out here. I hope
that you got the last parcel
from Tryanth allright, h...
have not had a letter in...
yet not up to the time of
writing this. but it hardly times

---

christmas for it will soon be
here now. I should like a new
... you can send me one we get
plenty of tobacco, but we have
not had any here since we stated
so you can tell how I could do with
one. Remember me to them all of
time and give the luck a hro and the
... a cuddle for me and good luck for
... your loving husband, Charlie
... A C Carruthers 9306 A co 9 th Batt
... a c Rest 13 division 39th Brigade
British Med Exped Force

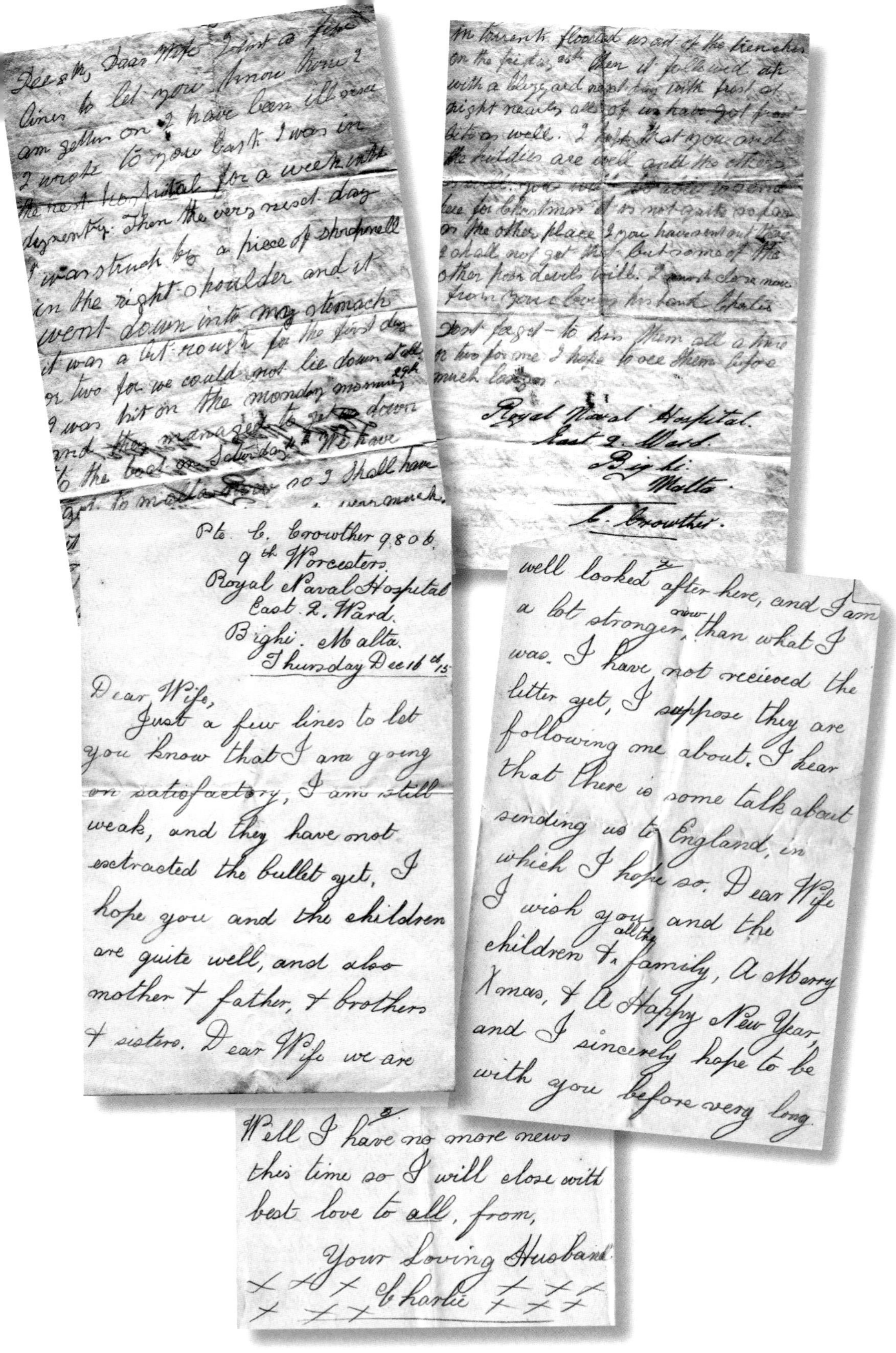

[Handwritten letter — multiple fragments]

Dec 8th Dear Wife, I just a few
lines to let you know how I
am getting on. I have been ill since
I wrote to you last. I was in
the next hospital for a week with
dysentery. Then the very next day
I was struck by a piece of shrapnell
in the right shoulder and it
went down into my stomach.
It was a bit rough for the first day
or two for we could not lie down at all
I was hit on the Monday morning
and they managed to get me down
to the boat on Saturday. We have
... so I shall have
... near much.

... torrent flooded us out of the trenches
on the Friday and then it followed up
with a blizzard and nearly froze us first of
night nearly all of us have got frost
bite as well. I hope that you and
the kiddies are well, and the others
... here for Christmas it is not quite so far
on the other place you haven't out there
we shall not get that but some of the
other poor devils will. I must close now.
From your loving husband Charlie
Don't forget to kiss them all a time
or two for me I hope to see them before
much longer.

Royal Naval Hospital.
East 2. Ward.
Bighi.
Malta.
C. Crowther.

Pte C. Crowther 9806.
9th Worcesters
Royal Naval Hospital
East 2. Ward.
Bighi. Malta.
Thursday Dec 16th/15

Dear Wife,
Just a few lines to let
you know that I am going
on satisfactory, I am still
weak, and they have not
extracted the bullet yet. I
hope you and the children
are quite well, and also
mother & father, & brothers
& sisters. Dear Wife we are

well looked after here, and I am
a lot stronger now than what I
was. I have not recieved the
letter yet, I suppose they are
following me about. I hear
that there is some talk about
sending us to England, in
which I hope so. Dear Wife
I wish you and the
children & all the family, A Merry
Xmas, & A Happy New Year,
and I sincerely hope to be
with you before very long.

Well I have no more news
this time so I will close with
best love to all, from,
Your Loving Husband
x x x Charlie x x
x x

Dear Wife 3/1/16

Just a few lines to let you know
that I am getting a bit stron
-ger I have not been the operation yet, but they have
had the X Rays on me twice
I dont think they can trace
the bullet yet. It has healed
up in my shoulder where
it went in I cant feel anything at all from that. I dont
think you had better send
anything else out there it
might get lost. like the other
stuff that has been sent out.
There were two transports sunk
with parcels and letters before
I got hit so suppose mine
was amongst the lot.
I have had a letter from
Mr Cozy tell dad to Remember
me to him I hope that you
and all the kids keep well
I should like to see them

again This letter must do for
you all this time for I cant
write very well yet it
makes my fingers ache doing
this bit. That was the first
letter I have had since the
day we sailed it was very
welcome. Let me know
what Brigade Arthurs lot
have joined Tell mother
and dad I cant write
this week but I hope you
will me have plenty of
news now. Remember me to
alice and all the lot of
them. Good night and
God bless you all till I
get over there again. give
all the kids a good kiss
and tell them to be good.
Your loving husband
Charlie
Pte C. Crowther 9386.
9th Worcester Regt.
Royal Naval Hospital
Bighi, Malta

Postscript

Charles' letters have been with me all my life. As a child I was allowed to cut the stamps off the Malta letters; they are still in my first stamp album. I was born twenty-two years after Charles died, and by then the letters were in the family bureau in a toffee tin. As I grew up, went to university and then married, I forgot them. By the time I had inherited all sorts of family papers I began to think that I ought to read the letters, but was daunted by their near illegibility from fading, tears and the general passage of time. Over the last year or two I have become very wrapped up in the Crowther family history, and both my son and I have been in touch with Lippett connections in Australia and Canada who were all keen to know more about Eliza's descendants. Suddenly I had a burning desire to read the letters, and get to know my grandfather. My long-suffering husband began the painstaking job of scanning them, and curiosity became obsession. I could not leave it there; I wanted to give Charles Crowther more than four medals, a gravestone and his name on a war memorial. How pleased I was that in 1969 we had given our son the names Charles and Crowther as his two middle names. As Al says in his foreword, this is the story of one ordinary man, his family and his friends as he made his tragic journey into the unknown. Charles was an ordinary man who did extraordinary things, but within his times he was also every man.

My grandparents' children all turned out well. Though dogged by misfortune, Wilfred succeeded at life despite his lack of education. He had to go to work as soon as he was ten, in order to provide income for the family. At first he had at least four jobs at any one time, since no one had full-time work to offer to a child. His mental arithmetic skills were mind-boggling. He explained the arithmetic away as the result of having worked as a bookie's runner very early on. Eventually he became a master roller of repute, an outstanding cricketer, captaining the Wilden side for many years, and a football coach.

Marjorie performed brilliantly in her school certificate at Kidderminster Girls' High School. She was in the top handful of candidates in the county. Unable to take up a place at university because there was a limit to how much Wilfred could earn, she buckled down as a trainee teacher. It took her most of her working life to reach the point of being recognised as qualified by the state and paid accordingly, yet during that time she was admired near and far for her inspirational teaching. She never bemoaned her fate; like my father, she just got on with things, eventually having a spell as Headmistress of the village school. Marjorie became fascinated with photography from an early age; Harry taught her all he knew and she went on to win a national competition. She developed all her own photographs, and we have been left with literally hundreds of shots of the youngsters as they grew up; we have Girl Guides, Boy Scouts, Girls' Friendly Society, Red Cross, Wilden Gymnastics Club, fancy dress parties at the vicarage and skating on a frozen Wilden Pool. She has left us a wonderful photographical record of Charles' children as they pulled together and survived.

Arthur was always a loner; Wilfred christened him Cruse (short for Crusoe). I talked to Arthur about that just before he died; he said it was a mystery to him why he was so good at football and cricket, because he was not inclined to teams and bonding, much preferring his own company. He excelled at athletics, and when his old school, Queen Elizabeth I Grammar School, Hartlebury, burned down some years ago, at least two of his records had still not been broken. About twenty years ago, a farmer with fields adjoining the school grounds ploughed up a mouldy cricket ball an impossibly long way from the school pitch; it was thought, after reference to old records, to have been one which Arthur hit out of the cricket ground and well across the next field; it had been assumed to be lost forever. Arthur was an outstanding all-round sportsman at school, and had he wanted could have had a professional career in a range of sports. His heart was not in it, though he did have a shot at it. When he was seventeen, Stafford Rangers FC were beaten to signing him and he played a trial season for Arsenal instead. He also played briefly for Aston Villa. After that he became a schoolmaster for a while, teaching mathematics and French, and then went to work for a local carpet company in their wages department, where he stayed till retirement. His work was interrupted by the Second World War, and he served with distinction with the Worcestershire Regiment in Egypt.

Betty was a brilliant cook and needlewoman (her various creations caused great envy amongst my university friends). She was also a gifted pianist and organist, with an infectious enthusiasm for poetry which had a great influence on me; as a young teenager I loved matching her quote for quote from our favourite poet, Rupert Brooke. She was the family homemaker, and a huge part of my life. I still use many of her handwritten recipes, and we could not have Christmas without her mincemeat!

Louisa undertook a seven-year hairdressing apprenticeship and ended up with her own business. She was a talented dancer, excelling at tap dance, and appeared in many local shows. As a very small child watching her in rehearsal, I thought her the most glamorous thing I had ever seen. She moved to Liverpool after marriage, and eventually became an honorary grandmother to my young son when we also moved there some thirty years later.

My grandmother coped with extraordinary dignity and courage, and felt great pride in her children. At the same time it must have been heartbreaking to see Wilfred, a very promising young scholar, miss out on so much as he strove to earn enough to supply endless Girl Guide and Boy Scout uniforms, school uniforms, cricket gear, football boots and so on. Marjorie did her best, but she was earning a pittance. By his mid-teens, Wilfred was deemed strong enough to go to work in the rolling mills of Wilden Ironorks. It was a rough, tough life in the mills, and he always remembered how kind and protective the men were of him as he grew up and learned to cope with the work and with the workforce there. One man who gave him much sound advice and talked to him a lot about Charles was Albie Downton, who lived long in Wilfred's memory. Albie and Charles had been pall-bearers together at Alfred's funeral, had known each other well and had worked together. Life had one last sting in the tail for my father though. Having seen all his siblings well educated and safely launched as adults, and having turned down the longed-for offer of a place on the ground staff at Worcester County Cricket Club because it did not pay as much as the rolling mills, he finally felt free to marry my mother after a ten-year wait. (She also had had a family to help financially). Five years later my mother was dead… and I was barely three. Whatever the tragedy in life, there are often pluses of a sort if you look for them. Because my father worked shifts, was deeply shocked and was also heavily committed to the Home Guard (this was the early 1940s), I went to live with my grandmother and Aunt Marjorie, by now living a couple of doors away from my great-aunts, Alice and Susie. Daily contact with all their family knowledge (and two of them were inspiring teachers), plus my father's tales at weekends, gave me a rare family knowledge which few people are lucky enough to have, hence much of the contents of Part One of this book.

I have tried very hard to be accurate and to err on the side of economy of detail where it is difficult to verify facts. Over the course of a century, during much of which data-storing facilities as we know them were not available, many things are impossible to check. All the Crowther, Mayall, Tipper and Bourne relatives of my father's generation who might have been able to help are dead. Even my grandfather's actual service record was lost in Second World War bombing. I hope readers will be tolerant if they spot an error.

Wilfred and Marjorie were old enough to absorb and remember what happened in 1916. However, with the passage of time, memory might have become dulled were it not for various meetings with Stanley Baldwin and his son Windham in later years, when the Baldwins had moved away from Wilden House and Wilden. Stanley had made his main home in Astley by the 1940s; this was the village where Alfred and William had first met in the 1860s. In 1944 Stanley, now retired, wrote to Wilfred, inviting him to 'bicycle over to Astley for tea and a chat.' During the next year or two, until Stanley's death in 1947, Wilfred cycled several times to Stanley's house and the two men simply sipped tea and talked of Wilden in years past, and recalled the people of Charles' and Stanley's generation. A decade later, Stanley's son, Windham, by then Earl Baldwin, wrote two very fine books. The first, published in 1956, was entitled *My Father, the True Story* and was triggered by a less than generous biography of his father. The second, *The Macdonald Sisters*, published in 1960, was about Louisa and her redoubtable sisters. Windham had a number of happy sessions with both Wilfred and Marjorie, checking facts about relationships, people and village life in general when both sets of grandparents set up home in Wilden and brought up their children there, and later watched their grandchildren grow. When Windham gave copies of the books to Wilfred and Marjorie, he wrote inside the front covers, 'In memory of the long friendship between our grandfathers' and 'In memory of old Wilden days.' These meetings were crucial in helping to keep memories sharp for all concerned. The two books have been invaluable to me both as reference aids and as fascinating reading material, full of Baldwin family minutiae.

I have always been fascinated by the deep and long friendship between Alfred Baldwin and my great-grandfather, William. I have several books inscribed, 'To my dear friend William Crowther', and ones similarly signed by Louisa and Stanley. Before I left home for university, putting flowers on various family graves was a weekly ritual; I always wondered what William looked like, and have wished that we had a photograph. Not long before the deadline for my book was due, I had a sudden compulsion to sort through an odds and ends drawer in my bedroom. I came across a locket which I knew had been Eliza's: it was pinchbeck and dull from wear. I had not thought about it for years. There was a tiny painted picture inside which I knew was William, but no one had ever really investigated it, believing it to be painted on a bit of glass, dull and dirty with age and not really suitable for enhancing. I rushed off to a photographer friend and asked him to take the locket apart and see if he could do anything. He gently removed what proved to be a tiny, exquisite, painted miniature of William; it was almost certainly done at the time of his marriage to Eliza in 1868, probably through the good offices of Alfred, in whose house William and Eliza were living. The locket's protective glass had been dirty rather than the painting dull. It has been a joy to include an enlarged scan of it at the beginning of this book. A happy knock-on effect was that it enabled me to identify one of Harry's glass negatives almost certainly as William, and to assume that the house behind him is the coach house. A photograph of William in later life has very recently been made available to me by the present Earl Baldwin, and one can see that not only was the miniature a good likeness, but bears a marked resemblance to both Susie and Charles' brother, Philip.

I have shed many tears over my grandfather's letters; for the waste of life; for the family heartache; for the unnecessary problem of late and inadequate pay; for the sending of a desperately weak man from a hospital bed straight into the firing line in below zero temperatures with no trench to take cover in; and not least for the way my lovely father's life was jolted off course. On the other hand, I am so proud of my grandfather's love for county, king and country. I applaud his total inability to 'whinge', and the objectivity of his letters home, omitting graphic details which he would not have felt his family could deal with as they passed his letters round, and yet conveying a real picture of how it was.

When I first walked around Bighi and looked out to sea across Valletta harbour, I had a thought which caused me almost more pain than anything else. I realised how alien that place would seem to an ordinary Englishman, dying there with no family or close friends to hand. How very different from Wilden. A world away.

Stanley Baldwin and Harry Cory in 1930. Although Stanley's mother was dead, his aunt Edith was still at Wilden House, and Wilden was always his special place to come home to.

Wilfred with his bride, Emily Bagnall, at St John's Church, Kidderminster, in 1936. Arthur was best man, and Dora Kate stands between her two sons. Louisa was bridesmaid, together with Emily's sister, Nell.

Dora Kate with her first grandchild, Ann, in 1939.

Stanley Baldwin and Canon Cory in 1936. Harry was now an honorary Canon of Worcester Cathedral. This is almost certainly early autumn, and it has always been thought locally that Stanley came home then for a day or two at this point to wrestle with the problem of the abdication, particularly the announcement to the public.

Laura and William
(Shammy) Bourne on
their golden wedding
anniversary in 1941.

Opposite from top
Almost the entire Bourne and Crowther family members gathered in Wilden for the golden wedding
anniversary. William is seated between Dora Kate and Laura, Canon and Mrs Cory are extreme left on
the front row, with Marjorie behind Mrs Cory in a dark dress. Emily and Wilfred with Betty are sixth,
seventh and eighth from the left at the back. A very small, bored Ann is extreme left on the children's
row. Arthur was away fighting in Egypt.

This is a small section of Wilden Home Guard in 1944. Wilfred is extreme right front row, with Bill
Bourne, his cousin, behind him, extreme right.

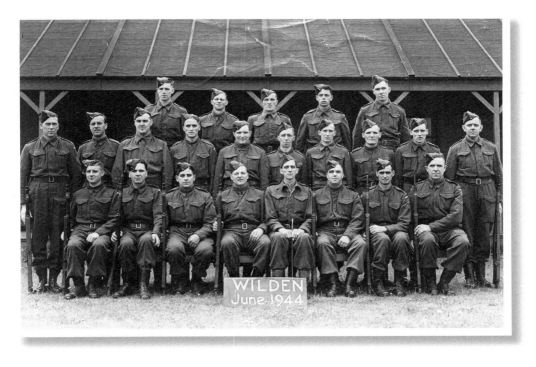

List of Names

Alfred Baldwin	Father of Stanley, husband of Louisa
Alice Crowther	Charles' elder sister
Arthur Bourne	Dora Kate's nephew, son of Shammy and Laura
Arthur Crowther	Charles' younger son
Astley	Village near Shrawley
Baldwin, Mrs	Louisa, wife of Alfred, mother of Stanley
Betty Crowther	Charles' middle daughter
Bewdley	Ancient small town on the Severn, three miles from Stourport
Bill Tipper	Dora Kate's uncle, a builder
Bill Tipper	Dora Kate's cousin (Bill's son)
Bert Cope	Friend of Charles, played for Hoobrook Olympic. He was also at Gallipoli and thought to be shell-shocked.
Charles 'Charlie' Crowther	Husband of Dora Kate
Coombeswood	Rural area north of Halesowen
Dick Bradley	Charles' friend, serving in France
Dora Kate Crowther, née Mayall	Wife of Charles
Eliza Crowther, née Lippett	Charles' mother
Frank Crowther	Charles' youngest brother
Fred Rosser	Charles' friend and a Wilden man; killed in action in France, with the Rifle Brigade.
George Crowther	Charles' brother, lived away from Wilden
Glover, Nurse	On staff at Bighi, Alice's friend
Guests	Harry Crowther's next-door neighbours
Harry Bourne	Shammy's youngest son
Harry Crowther	Charles' brother, father of Mollie
Hartlebury	Village near Wilden; Hartlebury Castle was home to the Bishops of Worcester for 1,000 years (now a county museum).
Jack Mayall	Dora Kate's younger brother
Jack Tipper	Dora Kate's nephew

Kate	(See Dora Kate)
Kathleen Fisher	On hospital staff at Bighi
Kidder, Kiddy	Kidderminster, the local market town
Laura Bourne, née Mayall	Dora Kate's sister
Lippetts	The family of Charles' mother
Louisa Baldwin	(See Baldwin, Mrs)
Louisa 'Louie' Crowther	Charles' infant daughter
Lower Mitton	Parish of St Michael's, Stourport
Marjorie Crowther	Oldest daughter of Charles
Martley	Village south of Shrawley, west of Worcester; the Crowthers had family there
Mayalls	The family of Dora Kate's father
Marian 'Mollie' Crowther	Harry Crowther's small daughter
Phillip Crowther	Charles' brother, working away from Wilden
'Shammy' (William Bourne)	Dora Kate's brother-in-law
Shrawley	William Crowther's birthplace, near Stourport
Stanley Baldwin	Son of Alfred and Louisa
Stourport-on-Severn	Small town a mile and a half from Wilden
Susan 'Sue'/'Susie' Crowther	Charles' younger sister
Syd and Sarah Mayall	Dora Kate's brother & his wife
Tippers	The family of Dora Kate's mother
Torton	Hamlet near Wilden and Hartlebury
Wilden	The Crowther village from 1870
Wilfred Crowther	Charles' elder son, known as Tim
William 'Bill' Bourne	Shammy's son, Wilfred's cousin and lifelong friend
William Henry 'Harry' Cory	Vicar of Wilden, later Canon Cory
William Crowther	Charles' father

Bibliography

The MacDonald Sisters by A.W. Baldwin (Peter Davies)

My Father, the True Story by A.W. Baldwin (George Allen & Unwin Ltd)

Our Inheritance by Stanley Baldwin (Hodder and Stoughton)

Service of our Lives by Stanley Baldwin (Hodder and Stoughton)

Earl Baldwin's Country by Byford-Jones (Wilding and Son)

The Worcestershire Regiment in the Great War by Captain H. FitzM Stacke (G.T. Cheshire & Sons Ltd)